Lives of a Gem!

God's Treasured Possession

Juel A. Fitzgerald

Juel's Creations, LLC

Beachwood, Ohio

Juel's Creations, LLC
P. O. Box 221172
Beachwood, OH 44122
https://juelscreations.wordpress.com/

Publisher's Note: This is a work of nonfiction. However, some of the names, persons, places, and incidents are based on the author's account or memory. Some individual's names have been changed.

Book Layout © 2017 BookDesignTemplates.com

Book Cover © 2020 designed by Andre A. Morgan, III.

Book Title/ Author Name. -- 1st ed.
ISBN 978-1-7348583-0-3

Acknowledgements

This book exists because of God. Through His Holy Spirit He prompted me to write these pages. He gave me a great support team before I began to write.

He gave me my husband, Danny, who supports me in whatever I do even when it seems crazy.

He gave me my parents, James and Kathryn, who have been in my corner since conception.

He gave me an editor, Amanda Kelsch, who lead me in the way I should go with this book. While I was still writing, she read Chapter One. She redirected me down a better path. Later she reviewed the completed manuscript while raising children and writing her own book.

He gave me a second editor, Derek Dixon, who reviewed added and modified chapters.

He gave me Andre A Morgan, III, Graphic Designer, to create the book cover.

Thank you, God, for leading me in Your way and not mine.

Table of Contents

Prologue

I have been writing another book that is a fictional novel for thirteen years. The first three chapters of this fiction originated in one of my creative writing classes while attending Kent State University. That creation now has twelve chapters completed. It has been a hard book to write.

On November 26, 2017, I heard a sermon given by Tom Caswell, a visiting pastor from our Worcester Massachusetts Church of Christ. His sermon was entitled "God's Peculiar People – His Treasured Possessions." God's Word reminded me that I am His and precious in His sight. Satan attempts to convince me that I am worthless, a piece of trash, nothing. I knew God loved me, but I never thought about being His Treasured Possession.

For at least a year before this sermon, God had prompted me through His Word, people and in other ways to write my story. But Satan kept saying, "Juel, who wants to read your story?" "You are a nobody." "Only famous people do that, who are you?" "What is so great about YOUR story?" "Your husband is part of your story and he is not ready."

The day of Tom's message from the pulpit, I heard the Holy Spirit say, "Put the fiction aside for now and write your story." I know the fiction will be finished, but on God's time; God never starts a work without finishing it.

At the age of sixty-four there have been many lives of Juel. Only two people know those lives completely – God and my husband. My dad knows most of them, but a few of them he never met. Each life could be a book by itself; this journey will touch on most of them.

CHAPTER ONE

THE YOUNGSTER

"Very truly I tell you, when you were younger you
dressed yourself and went where you wanted."
John 21:18a.

I was born a snob. I was not the stereotypical African American. Both of my parents were government workers. My dad, James Jr., was a U.S. Post Office letter carrier and my mom, Kathryn, worked at several government agencies – Department of Defense and VA Hospital come to mind. It was their aim for my younger brother, Jimmy, (James, III.), and me to have a life that was better than theirs. And it was!

Neither of my parents lived a wealthy life. My dad had three siblings – two sisters and a brother. Dorothy was the oldest, dad was next, Louise was third and Claude fourth. A great deal of their lives they lived in various foster homes while dad's mom was sick. His father could not take care of the four of them and work. Dad's mom died when he was nine years old. His dad was born in North Carolina, moved to Cleveland where he married, and all the children were born. Aunt Dorothy had one child, Deborah. Aunt Louise had one child, Christine. Uncle Claude married Dorothy and had three daughters, Rosalind, Leslie and Stacey. I had fun growing up with these cousins. Deborah, Rosalind and I were closest because we were all close in age; the others were too young to play with.

My mother had six siblings: Ethel, Adele, Florence, Helen, Chester and Lester (the latter two were fraternal twins); mom was number five of seven. She was born in Cape Girardeau, MO. I am thinking all her siblings were born there too, but I am not sure. Her dad, Helen, Lester, Chester and my mom moved to Chicago after her mother died to be near where her mother's sister lived. Adele, Ethel and Florence were grown by that time. Adele lived in Denver. She had three sons: Albert, Nathaniel and Rodney. Ethel lived in California and had ten children: Darryl, Terry, Pat, Penny, Jerome, Kathy, Clyde, Leonard, Michelle and Don. I was closest to Kathy, Jerome and Clyde; we were close in age. Florence lived in Chicago and had a daughter, Chris and a son, Allen.

My mother's father, Napoleon, met Ruth at church in Chicago. Soon after marrying they moved to her hometown in Cleveland. This was the grandfather and step grandmother I knew. I never knew Ruth was my mother's stepmother until I was older. Every time I think about her I think about the time she served my brother and I dinner. She plopped a whole pig's foot on my plate. I gagged. It had the nails on it! I had never eaten pig's feet. She cried out, "How are you being raised that you never had pig feet?! I am going to have to talk to your mom about this!" I did not eat it either. It looked gross! A foot on my plate?! Seriously?

Mom's other siblings also had children. Helen had three sons – Stoney (Melvin, Jr.), Milton and Melton (fraternal twins). Chester had two girls – Christina and Crystal (fraternal twins). Lester had three children – Chevelle, Melanie and Lester.

My parents met in Sunday school. My dad was two and a half years older than my mom. She was fifteen and he, eighteen at the time. He had no interest in her. Then one day in February 1953, he was crossing the street after church heading to work to wash trucks. My mom called, "James!" Dad turned around; this girl he knew in Sunday school had grown up. He crossed back across the street and they had a conversation. The very next day, Dad got a notice in the mail. He had seventeen days to report to the Army; he had been drafted. My mom and dad had a quick courtship in those seventeen days. During the next four to five months they wrote each other every day. After he completed boot camp and got stationed, they were officially boyfriend and girlfriend. They were married September 11, 1954 while Dad was stationed at Fort Niagara. He came home every other weekend, even if he didn't have a pass. He managed to get passes from soldiers who could not go home and used theirs to get home to Cleveland by bus, train or hitch hiking. He was discharged February 1955. While Dad was in the service, my mom rented an efficiency down the street from her parents. Being married and out from under her parents was the best thing that had happened to her.

I lived in four houses with my parents. They were in my Uncle Melvin's and Aunt Helen's home, a shared duplex, my parents' two-family house and my parents' bungalow. All four of the homes were in Cleveland, OH. I never knew what it was like to live in a rented apartment. My parents stayed with my uncle and aunt when I was born on Lipton Avenue. My memories of that dwelling were after we moved out while we lived in my parents' homes. Stoney, their oldest son, and I were the same age; we were two babies in my aunt's house. The twins came a few years later.

This three-bedroom house with a living room, bathroom, kitchen with a dinette area on the first floor and an open full basement will always be the place of my first painful injury. I sprained my ankle by falling down the stairs at their front door to the outside. Jimmy, my brother, and I spent lots of time playing with our three cousins in their house and up and down the street with their friends. That is where I had my first "show me yours and I will show you mine" game with my cousins in the closet. We got caught. Whack!

Whack! "Don't you ever do that again!" My Aunt Helen's hard hand sent flames into my behind. "I won't! I won't! I'll be good!" I cried. To this day I cannot remember if she told my parents. She probably did, and they had a good laugh about it.

My parents shared a duplex with my Aunt Louise and Uncle Claude. I remember nothing about this white with teal trimmed house. My Aunt Louise showed me the house when I was sixty-three years old. She asked me to take her on a ride of the old neighborhood to see what had changed. This house was still there, unlike other places she grew up in that had been torn down. I remember seeing a black and white childhood picture of me in the back yard of a place I did not know. After seeing this place with my aunt, it confirmed where that picture was taken.

My parents bought their first home on East 116th Street. It was a two-family up and down. Sometimes we lived upstairs; sometimes we lived downstairs. The other half was rented out to family and friends. I loved living upstairs best because it was closest to our huge attic which we used as a play area. My brother and I used one of the large storage spaces behind the walls as a playhouse. One of my favorite things to do was to people-watch from the upstairs down to the street. The basement was an open space the size of the house with two cement sinks, a wringer washing machine and furniture to sit on. A corner, near the stairs, was enclosed by a wall with a locked door that my father built. This room was for his TV repair business. He always did something on the side. Later in life, he worked full time at Ford while still working full time at the post office. Making money was his goal; we were never in want.

In this house, my parents had dance and card parties. It amazes me how playing bid whist was part of our household, but I never learned. Actually, I didn't want to learn. My parents' friends and family were so competitive that they belittled anyone who made a mistake. I did not want any parts of that game! "Why did you make that play?!" "Help me out here! We are supposed to be partners!" "Next time, remind me not to pick you as my partner!" Our house was never quiet. With my grandfather and other family living there, there was always something going on and someone there. That is probably why I liked the attic; I could escape there for solitude. I had four males in my life whom I loved, but I did not always want to be around. All four were alcoholics – my grandfather and three uncles. When they were over, I tried to be out of the way, if I was allowed. Though they were the coolest people when sober, they were not fun when drunk.

If I was not in the attic, I was outside playing in the streets with neighborhood friends. My best friend, Cheryl, and I were always together. We spent many overnighters at each other's houses laying "butty to butty" and laughing about that. She had a huge brown Great Dane that I was terrified of. He did not like anyone coming into their house. Wham! Gigantic brown nailed paws slammed on the security door; teeth, slobber and ear-piercing bass barking greeted me. "Come get him and let me in!" I screamed. He was restrained when I stayed over but I had nightmares of him getting me. I am surprised I do not have a fear of dogs. Cheryl and I were friends with everyone on the street. We had no fear of walking alone in our neighborhood. Our only persecutors were the "Whip Boys." They were boys up to no good.

"Run! Here they come!" Cheryl or I would cry out and dash off away from them.

It makes me wonder, now, who they were, what their stories were and what became of them.

I never thought about our neighborhood not being safe, until the race riots. In the summer, my parents always shipped us to North Carolina to stay with family. One of those times, in the South, I was watching news on TV about the race riots in Cleveland. "Hold up! That is near where we live! Oh my gosh! Is Mommy and Dad ok?" I jumped up. "I gotta call them now!"

"We are ok, baby. The fires are not close to us at all! Yes, we will be careful!" Our parents were relieved we were somewhere safe away from the chaos.

I was saddened when my dad bought another house. I was going to be separated from my best friend and all the friends I knew. However, after I got a chance to see the bungalow on East 116th Street, in what I considered a swank neighborhood, I was thrilled. With nose upturned, I told everyone, "We are moving to a house that has TWO patios, TWO bathrooms and a TWO-car garage!" Our corner house bungalow on East

116th and Avon Avenue had a full basement with a spare bathroom. My dad built a recreation room with a wet bar in later years for parties. The first floor had the standard living room, kitchen, dinette area, bathroom and two bedrooms. My brother and I had bunk beds in the front bedroom and my parents in the back room. The upstairs was a full attic. Soon my father built a bedroom and an open room with behind-the-wall storage space like we had at our first home. The upstairs soon became my brother's bedroom. He also put in two built-in desks for us to study in that attic. This was the first house I saw that had carpeting in the kitchen – a yellow and brown plaid. Every room in the house was huge!

We had a wine cellar in the basement. It went to great use. Every year we would pluck the grapes in our backyard over the furthest patio and make wine. The smell of fermenting grapes filled the house along with white spiders. I hated those white spiders! We also had a huge garden. Fresh corn on the cob was my favorite. We shucked many ears of corn. "Yuck! There is a worm in this corn! Get it out!" As an adult, I still slowly peel back the husks waiting to see a wiggly worm.

Family lived in this house like they did in the first house; it was a shared experience. One day, my mom's sister Adele died. My parents moved her three sons from Denver to Cleveland. It was a changed life – an increase from two children to five. It was good, but at times it was not good. Eventually, my parents could not handle five children, especially with the youngest having a mental handicap. In those days, my cousin, Rodney was labeled as retarded. My cousins had to be placed in foster homes. I felt bad about that, but happy we had our house back; it was bittersweet. Thanks, to God, I was reunited with them as adults with the added blessing of meeting Nate's children. Dad and I were able to meet regularly with Rodney for lunch; he died in his 50's. Albert left Cleveland; his whereabouts are unknown.

Since both of my parents were government workers, we traveled a lot! We drove everywhere! We drove to places from the Atlantic to the Pacific Ocean. We drove north to Niagara Falls regularly. If Mexico had been closer and safer, we probably would have driven there. I saw the Grand Canyon when I was a teenager. I realized later as an adult that when I was a teen, the Grand Canyon and many other places we drove to were mere notches on a list of places I had been. I loved to travel as a child, but I did not see the beauty in those places until I was older.

My father journalized all our trips. I must have inherited his love of writing. I started a journal when I was eight years old. Every detail of my day including conversations in quotes were in those early journals. I often wondered how I had time to write all that and be active in school. I was active in writing, running track, cheering as a high school booster, editor of the high school newspaper and other activities. I was a nerd! I took college preparation courses and vocational classes in typing and shorthand. I attended summer school for at least two summers to maintain this class schedule. I had friends, but I was not popular. I remember writing novels and submitting them to various publishers. I was always rejected! As an adult, I can see why. They were not professional – misspellings, untidy and sometimes single-spaced. Who wanted to read that?

My parents rarely spared the rod. Belts snatched through pants loops disciplined us into obedience. Once when I was between ten and twelve years old, I was playing in the basement by myself with candles. Do not ask me why, maybe I was a growing pyro. Anyway, I lit up a bunch of them; I liked watching the fire and the smell. I still love campfires as an adult. Before my parents got home, I cleaned up the mess and aired out the room.

"Juel, were you playing with matches in the basement?" my dad asked.

"No," I answered. *I wasn't playing with matches. I was playing with candles, even though I did use a match.* I thought.

"Were you burning candles?" *Candles? Why would he ask that? I left no evidence.*

"No, not me."

"Are you sure?"

"Yep."

"Let me show you something." He took me down into the basement. On the wet bar were gobs of melted candle wax. Busted.

"You know playing with matches are dangerous in the house. If you had told the truth, it would not have been so bad for you. But because you lied, you are getting a whooping!" He tore my behind up. Normally by this time belt whippings did not hurt so much, and I would pretend to cry, but this one did. "I am sorry! I am sorry! I won't do it again!" My father assured me he still loved me, but that I should never lie.

I was incredibly quiet but not shy. I listened and watched; talking excessively was a waste of words to me. With a pen, words came out that I did not or could not speak. I was not crazy about being in crowds, however, it did not make me uncomfortable being in crowds. Yet, at the same time I was a loner. I was an active introvert.

Making and keeping friends was easy. Many of my girlfriends from kindergarten to twelfth grade are still close friends as adults. We have gone through much from boyfriends, husbands, children, illnesses, divorces and a death of one of them in our 60's. That first death within our group was hard, but God got us through it.

I liked boys, but I wanted to be a virgin when I married. I had a real boyfriend, late for most – around fifteen or sixteen years old. My mom loved him because he was handsome, probably because of the beautiful babies we could make. At one time, I thought he was the one. I was too young to know any different. We dated for two years. He made advances, but I denied them because I was saving myself for marriage. Somehow, he convinced me. I cannot remember why – maybe my fear of losing him. What I do remember is how mad he was at me afterwards.

"You whore!" His face was bright red.

"What??? I have not been with anybody!"

"Yes, you have! I waited all this time for nothin'! Get outta my face!"

I got dressed and left his house. It was some-time later before I realized why he accused me of that. There was no bloody show. I was an athlete. I chose to wear the new device called a tampon instead of a pad when I ran in a race. I hated those pads with the belt! "Can you see? Can you see?" I would ask my girlfriends. "No, girl, no one can see your pad!" The first time I tried this brand-new device for a track meet, it got stuck. It took me hours to get it out; it was too deep. I broke my virginity with a tampon! Despite that painful sit-uation, I never went back to pads.

"Are you and Joseph boyfriend and girl-friend?" a close classmate asked me while we were in the science lab dissecting a frog.

"Ahhhh, yeah." *The whole world knows that,* I thought.

Her face turned red and liquid filled her eyes. "I am so sorry! I am so sorry! He told me he didn't have a girlfriend and it was ok!"

"What are you talking about?" I did not know what else to say.

"He – he – we, we, we made love." Her voice trailed off.

Gasp! *What?* I thought. *So, that is what he did while he was waiting for me! Wow! AND he accused ME of being a whore!*

My friend was more devastated than I to learn we were a couple. She was a shy person and did not have many school friends that I could see. I was stunned but felt sorry for her. I often wondered why she joined the Army instead of college when she had a full scholarship. She never explained why, even though I asked. I have never seen her again or heard anything about her. I do not even remember her name. I will always thank God that he spared me from marriage with that man. I am not sure if I was so numbed by this betrayal because I do not remember why I did not want to kill or accuse him of what I had learned. Maybe because after he called me a whore, in my mind, I was walking away from him anyway and this news sealed it.

Besides the infidelity, I was almost choked to death by him in my house for something he got mad at me for. I felt myself passing out and only God made him stop. That was scary. I never told anyone except a few people later in life and my future husband. I did not have anything to do with him after that.

I dated one other guy after that; we were not a couple – just a one-time fling. I learned about female erogenous zones through him. Even though it was not all that great for me, it led me to read up on what sex should feel like between females and males. Next time I was going to be prepared!

My acceptance to Kent State University was the first step toward my plan to be a journalist.

However, I wanted a summer job before I left for school. I had only worked one job before graduating. It was a telemarketing job in Northfield, OH across the street from the racetrack. I was only there two days before I quit. Being locked up in a windowless room calling strangers on a quota was not for me. My parents were probably glad because they had to drive me there and it was far from home. I am surprised they let me have that job.

As government employees, my parents steered me toward the government. I was hired as a full-time permanent clerk for the Navy Finance after graduation. I wanted a summer only job, but there was none to be had for a person who had no experience. I took the bus to the Federal Building downtown to do clerical work to make sure soldiers got paid. I loved this first job; I discarded that first telemarketing one as not a job. I almost wished I did not have to leave when I quit late in the summer to go to school. I told them I changed my mind and planned to go to school instead. That was my plan all along; I took the position to earn some money before leaving for Kent. My employer was not happy because I was only there for two, maybe three months. I did not care; going to Kent State was my goal. I had to do what I had to do.

CHAPTER TWO

THE COLLEGE STUDENT

"Now the Berean Jews were of more noble character than those in Thessalonica, for they received the message with great eagerness and examined the Scriptures every day to see if what Paul said was true." Acts 17:11

It took thirty-seven years to obtain a bachelor's degree in English. I wanted to be a journalist who traveled around the world. I was accepted at Kent State University and was excited about going to the school where the shootings had taken place. Wearing one of my KSU shirts in public was cool. "Wow! You go to that school where those kids got shot! Were you there then?" I almost wished I had been, so I could have a story to tell, which I know now is not a good way to think. So many were killed senselessly, and my young mind did not quite grasp what really happened and why. As an adult I have come to know one of the victims who remains in a wheelchair. I met him at a race that we both were in.

"Well, here is your dorm room!" my mom said. The door had some fancy welcome decoration on it.

"Look at that window! It is huge!" I pointed. Green grass beyond the parking lot and other buildings captured my eyes. *People watching, here I come!* I learned later that grassy area was near where the shootings took place. My dorm was a few steps away from Taylor Hall.

"This room is not bad at all!" Dad added. "I thought it was going to be small."

"I thought so too. We got bunk beds and two desks and lots of drawer space. Since my roommate is not here yet, I am taking the lower bunk." The blanket felt soft to my touch.

"What if she wants the lower bunk?" my mom asked.

"Well, I am ok if she wants the bottom one, just rather not have to climb that ladder every day or fall out the bed at night. Look at all this closet space. Mirrors, too, and a phone!"

"Let me copy that number down, so we can call you." Dad grabbed a pen from his front pocket and began to scribble.

"Do you need us to help you unpack?" Mom picked up one of the suitcases.

"No, I can do that. You guys gotta long drive back home."

"Ok, is there anything else you need?" they asked in unison.

"No." I pulled open drawers to see how much space was in them.

"Ok, I guess we should be leaving," whispered mom.

We all hugged. I felt some kind of way, but not sure what. "Let me walk down to the lobby with you."

More hugs in the lobby and they were gone. I strolled through the lobby and other public rooms on the first floor then took the elevator back up to my floor. In my room I gazed out the window. I claimed the desk by the window. A slow smile crepted on my face. I was alone in my own place; no, parents to contend with, just a roommate.

My roommate was white. She was a nursing student in her last year. How a freshman and a senior were assigned together is still a mystery. She did not want to live in an apartment but chose to stay in the dorm. She took the KSU bus into Cleveland for her training at one of the local hospitals. We were friends but did not spend time together. She was busy with finishing and I was starting my new freedom away from home. After the end of the second semester, we departed and never kept in touch. I assume she graduated and became a nurse.

The Kent State campus was huge. Walking the grounds or taking the loop bus was so much fun for me! I loved going to the area where the shootings were. It was a memory I could not relate to but found interesting. Hanging out with new friends, eating pizza, dancing and returning to my dorm whenever I wanted to, was the best!

Freshman year was short; I fell in love, got married and pregnant. My plans to be a journalist went out the window. I did not care. I would do something else and write.

"Girl, you need to go back to school and get some accounting if you want to move up here!" A coworker, years later when I was an employee of the Internal Revenue Service (IRS), said. "You don't want to be a file clerk forever!"

So, as a married woman with a young son, I returned to school. My accounting courses were taken at Cuyahoga Community College and Kent State in order to move up the ladder at the IRS. Once I got the minimum amount of accounting courses, I dropped out and worked. Being a Certified Public Accountant was not what I wanted to be; I wanted to write.

"Your writing is good, but you need to go back to school to hone your craft," my first editor told me about a book I was working on.

So, back to Kent State I traveled as a wife, mother of two adult children, one granddaughter and a full-time position with IRS, to study English. I took advantage of the regional campuses because it cost less to attend there than main campus. Stark Campus was my favorite. The hardest part was the long drive to and from, especially in the winter. All my classes were at night after work two to three days a week.

Staying awake on the highways was a chore. One night I was driving to Stark Campus. I remember passing an exit that was two exits from mine on Interstate 77 Southbound. As if in slow motion, my hands were turning right on their own; in the dark my eyes adjusted to what was happening. I was making a circular exit – the typical right turn exits into a big circle that ends on an overpass. It was so dark; I could not tell where I was. At the light, I had to stop. "Where the heck am I?" I was on the exit just before my exit. "How did I get here?" My knees trembled; my palms were wet. I must have fallen asleep. How could I have driven this exit in my sleep? I gasped for air! Oh my gosh! I could have been killed! I turned left on the street and drove the rest of the way to school on the side street. I was too scared to get back on the highway and drive to my exit. Every time I think about this, I thank God, because he was driving; I was not.

Taking classes online in the winter made it easier to take classes without fear of driving at night in the snow. The disadvantage was classes were never cancelled because of weather; it was also harder. The interaction with the teacher and the students typing discussion answers was intense, but I learned a lot and enjoyed being home while the snow fell outside.

"Are you planning to be a teacher when you graduate?" people would ask me when they heard what I was doing.

"No, I just want to write!" Teaching was fun, but I'd rather teach adults; I no longer had the patience to teach kids. "School is so expensive. How are you doing this?" someone would ask.

"Student loans," I sighed. "Somehow, God is going to work it out. He is the one who sent me back to school." I did not like the debt that was building up, but what was I to do? Payment plan or saving was not an option; there never was enough money to do that.

Finally, on May 7, 2011, when I was fifty-five years old, I graduated from Kent State with a bachelor's degree in English. My cousins from Maryland, nieces, children, granddaughter, husband and dad were there along with my best friend, Debra from California.

Maggie, a friend I met when we were Girl Scouts leader, came. As the cameras clicked away, she said, "Here, take this for all those years of school." She handed me a brown bear with a black graduation cap, and black shirt that read in white lettering, "Kent State Class of 2011." *This was happening! I made it!*

"Party over here!" Coworkers, family and friends celebrated with me at a party afterwards at a club that had rental space. We ate and danced the night away!

Thirty-seven years it took to get a bachelor's degree – in the same year I retired from IRS into a new life.

CHAPTER THREE

THE WIFE

*"A wife of noble character who can find?
She is worth far more than rubies."
Proverbs 31:10*

Love at first sight. That is what happened
when I saw Danny, a tall, dark, chocolate, with a
large afro, Senior.   I was a Senior, too, and had
never met him. We were in the cafeteria. He was
trying to get one of my girlfriends to take a chocolate milk out of the cafeteria in her purse for him;
we were not supposed to take food out of the cafeteria.   I teased him, "You can't do that!" We
joked around with each other as my friend took the
milk out for him before parting ways. I think I got
his name from my girlfriend.   In the next few
weeks, I looked for him; he walked right past my
stenographer class every day. I watched him pass,
but never spoke. He had a female locker mate;
they looked cozy like they were a couple. *It fig-
ures, he had someone.* I thought, *what is a good-*

looking guy like him doing with an ugly girl like her?! I was too afraid of her to even try to make any advances on him. I was not that kind of girl anyway – stealing from another. I had been hurt enough by it happening to me. Plus, he did not seem interested in me at all.

One day he did not pass by the class. I made sure I was standing outside that door every day just to see him, even if I could not have him. Then another day passed and several more. I wondered where he was. Then maybe a week later, I saw him approaching. I cried out, "Danny, where have you been?!" What was I thinking? This dude already had a girlfriend.

His eyes lit up and he stopped as if in shock. "I have been sick and stayed home." He answered in a proper tone that I was not accustomed to hearing.

"Oh, no wonder," I said.

In the weeks that followed, all my assumptions were proven wrong. First, the locker mate was an ex-girlfriend. They had dated briefly earlier in the year, but that was over. They had been assigned the same lockers because there were no other lockers available through their homeroom. We all shared lockers with someone – not enough lockers in the building. Second, the reason I had never seen him before was because he enrolled at John Adams High School in the twelfth grade. His parents had moved from Maple Heights to Cleveland. He spoke proper English because of his exposure to going to school with white people. But he knew how to talk street language when he needed to. Third, he was *very* interested in me. While I was watching him at every passing, he was watching me. He said he even tried to speak to me but got nowhere with me. I fail to remember anytime he tried to talk with me.

Soon we were going steady. He walked me home every day. We would sit on my parents' back porch and talk with our faces close to each other especially in the cold. My parents were still at work so I could not let him in the house and did not want to. For months we sat close enough to kiss, but only talked. We talked for hours on the phone late at night also. Then one day in March 1974 one or both of us leaned in and our lips met.

"Finally! I have been wanting to kiss you forever!" one of us said.

We both laughed and with lips flapping about how we could have sat that close all those months and not kissed. I cannot remember how it happened, but the next thing I knew we were both saying, "Let's get married!"

It was so natural to talk about our future. "Let's wait until we both finish school. I know my parents will not pay for going to Kent State if I get married too early," I said. I was looking forward to being away from my parents at Kent.

"For real. My parents will say we are too young, and we are. I want to go to school to learn electronics."

"How many kids do you want?" I asked.

"Five, I am used to a big family."

"Cool, I have always wanted to be in a big family." We talked on about our dreams as a married couple.

While I was at Kent State, we spent every weekend together. He drove up and stayed the whole weekend or I was home. I would ride the Kent State bus home to see him. It was a girl's dorm, but we managed to sneak him in, and he would stay overnight. My roommate knew he was there but did not mind. She was always gone in the morning, by the time we got up.

Then, I missed a period. Oh no! I was pregnant! Darn it! I was only a freshman for three months! We decided to elope. I wore a short white dress and Dan wore something dressy. We were married by Judge Kent in Kent, Ohio on November 8, 1974. We told no one, not even my roommate. We went home that day. His sister, Precious, saw me in that dress and said, "I got married in a dress like that!" We both laughed. We were going to wait until the pregnancy was obvious before we told anyone. Then my period came! I was not pregnant! "Oh well," we said, "We were going to get married anyway; it just happened sooner than planned." I kept going to school. He kept going to work with our secret. Going to electronic school did not quite pan out for him.

In the Spring of 1975, I got sick a lot; I missed a lot of classes. I finally decided to see the school nurse. I really was pregnant this time. I had to tell my parents. I had missed so much class that I had to drop out. I cannot remember if my parents were shocked, disappointed or what; I was too sick. When we told them we were already married, they did seem relieved. I still wanted a church wedding with the white gown and reception. Dan and I were members of the Calvary Pentecostal Church of God across the street from our old high school for at least a year. I still wanted to get married in the eyes of God. Our first marriage was the legal one and the second one would be the God one. So, with bun in the oven, we got married in the church on July 5, 1975.

Dan's parents, Owen and Jacqueline, especially his dad, were not too thrilled about us getting married so young. "You are doomed to divorce because you are too young!" His dad frowned. When they moved to Cleveland, he had warned Danny not to get involved with those "Cleveland" girls. One day while we were still dating, I biked my way to his house in my blue floppy hat and his dad was not happy. I was a "Cleveland" girl and not a light-skinned African American with red hair – not what he wanted for his son! However, after he discovered I could bake cakes from scratch and banana pudding pie, he loved me!

For a year and a half, we lived with my parents, worked and saved money to buy a house. This was a perfect arrangement economically; emotionally it was not. "You shouldn't do that, or you should do this . . ." our didn't-want-hear-it ears were filled with this. As inexperienced young adults of eighteen and nineteen, we wanted to do it on our own and were ready to move.

Our son, Danny Jr., was born while we lived under their roof. It was good having my mom to help me with this new addition to my life – an addition I had no experience with. However, as our son grew older, I was ready to leave because I could not really be a wife or a mother while still living with parents, who were helpful, but annoying at the same time. We purchased a two-story bungalow on a slab in Warrensville Heights in December 1976.

"Wooo whoo! We are outta here before Christmas!" I said after the papers were signed. We drove past our new house for weeks while the closing process took place. "Soon we will be there in our own place! I can hardly wait. We will be able to spend our first Christmas in our new house." Decorating our house for Christmas filled my thoughts.

This was our first time living on our own; it was liberating, and it was different. Now I had space to spread out. Our house had two bedrooms, a living room, bath, kitchen and dinette area on the first floor. Half of the second floor was a finished bedroom with a tiny closet; the other half was an unfinished attic – perfect for storage. The bedrooms on the first floor had huge closets with sliding door mirrors. It made each room look larger than they were. The kitchen was small, but it contained the stove, refrigerator and clothes washing machine that came with the house. The upper and lower cabinet space and counter space was small but seemed huge to me, then, because it was mine. Now I was no longer playing house but was a real wife.

We both continued to work and raise our son. I worked for the Veteran Administration Hospital as a Dietary Clerk. My mom worked there in the office area. When we were still living with them, I got a ride with her. Once we moved, I took the bus. I was taught what type diets patients needed to be on based on what their ailment was. Three of us sat in an office in the hospital kitchen and wrote out cards with a patient's name, room number and the type diet the kitchen had to serve. We also gave the kitchen the patient's food selection if they were on a regular diet. It was fun going up on the floors to collect the regular diet charts patients filled out. I worked there for a year. I accepted a clerical position with the Internal Revenue Service in the Federal Building downtown and left the kitchen.

Dan worked at Cook United, Ford, United Parcel and finally as a Journeyman Pipefitter at Local 120. All his jobs were union based. While working any of these positions Danny was laid off for various periods of time regularly. He made good money when he was working. When he was not working, we lived on unemployment and my job.

In the beginning having Dan home, caring for our son was perfect. This saved us money in babysitting. It gave him quality time with his son while I worked. Soon however, I began to get resentful. I did not want to be a working mother. I wanted to stay home, unlike my mom did. She worked and left us with sitters, or we were latch-key kids. I had dreams that when I grew up, I would be a stay at home mom for my kids. This was not turning out as I planned; I was turning into my mom. Dan was not always happy either while I worked, and he did not. Neither of us under-stood, then, man's need to be respected through employment. It was not his fault when he was laid off, but I wanted him to find a different job that would not put us in that situation. I could not un-derstand why he would not do that for me.

"You know I can't do that!" Dan would say when I suggested another way to work. "Any time someone sees where I have worked and how much money, they won't hire me. Because they know the minute I get called back, I am gone! Besides, I don't want to do any of those other types of jobs." It was only a matter of time before we both looked for contentment in the arms of another.

CHAPTER FOUR

THE ADULTRESS

*"Marriage should be honored by all, and the
marriage bed kept pure, for God
will judge the adulterer and all the sexually im-
moral." Hebrews 13:4.*

"We are so young, and we went straight from
living at home with our parents to being married.
I feel we have not had a chance to sow our wild
oats. Don't you think it would be a cool idea to
see other people sometime?" one of us said. I do
not remember whose idea this was, probably mine.
Dan is not very vocal, but obviously thought the
same.

With free love and wife swapping, the idea
was nothing new. We could stay married and gain
some experience to use in our marriage.

Attraction for me started in the workplace,
then expanded to other groups that I was active in.
Words of admiration tickled my ears. Flirting was
fun; I relished in the warmth of being admired by
a man. A kiss here and there was a part of that

temptation. Jumping on a handsome man's bones was not my first thought; in fact, I was not so sure I wanted to do all that. What would happen if I got pregnant? We still wanted more children. Sexual diseases never entered my mind. The problem with flirting and kissing is, it is almost impossible to stop there. Whether I wanted to go further or not, not many men wanted to stop there; at times, neither did I.

Having an open marriage at first was a thrill. The exposure to sexual pleasures were brought home for further enjoyment. "Now, I understand how a sex therapist works. This is cool, I got to help, Mark, with his relationship with Susie, by helping him to love her more in bed. Too bad, I couldn't get paid for this." Dan agreed as he grabbed me to teach me something he had learned.

It was not like we searched out for new conquests; we just did not fight off any that fell into our laps. Any time I traveled for work, those were perfect opportunities to have fun and party it up!

That dangling carrot turned into grief.

"You could have called me to say you were going to be out that long. I waited for hours for you. You had me worried."

"What do you see in her?"

"What do you see in him?"

"Gee, you are paying more attention to them than me."

"Don't you love me anymore?"

"You didn't tell me you were married. You let me fall in love with you and now I don't know what to do."

"Why are you not leaving your spouse for me? Aren't I giving you what they are not giving you at home? Why suffer when you can have me forever?"

"I worked all this time to get you and you say it is only about the sex! I thought you loved me!"

Heartache and regret became a part of our marriage. If we were not hurting each other, we were hurting the ones we fooled around with. "We need to stop this. This hurt! Let's go back to how it should be." We both agreed and ceased our consensual affairs for a time.

However, it was not long before someone would touch my arm in the right way and my eyes would gaze upon another man. "I am going to hang out with Sally." "I will be late at a travel agent meeting." "I will be late coming back from Scouting training." Lying was easy. I did not like the lying. I just needed to get away from home and be with someone I thought cared for me. I could tell Danny was sneaking out also. Infidelity is not easy to hide. The signs are obvious, the smells, the nonverbals, the dress, the change in behavior, changes in arrival/departure times, changes in speech, changes in emotions, and so on. It becomes of matter of whether the other party really wants to confront the situation or let it go.

I did not lack anything in my marriage, but I felt like I did because I was greedy. I had a husband who paid attention to me, made good money when he wasn't laid off, was patient with the children, where I was not, shared in household duties, was handsome, spoke excellent English, enjoyed doing the same fun things I liked to do and more. So, why I was never quite satisfied with my life then, is beyond me now. I was insatiable. I wanted his full attention and did not want to share. Once I knew we were both still playing the same games, then, it made it easier for me to justify my behavior. Having my cake and eating it too was harder because of the deceptions, but it was better than being home alone.

Several times we had a shared experience – another woman, me and Dan. I longed to be with Dan and another guy. It never happened. We came close, but God slammed that door shut hard; now I am grateful. The thought of orgies repulsed us, so, we did not go that far.

The word "divorce" never came up in our marriage until much later in life. Though I am sure we thought it, we never said it. "Maybe we could just separate and see how that works." We never did. Living in a separate place alone did not sound good to either of us. It would have been hard for me to fight off the guys I was hanging with, I wouldn't have been able to use my standby excuses "I am married with children. This can only go so far." "My husband won't give me a divorce."

Praises only to God, neither of us got HIV or any other sexual diseases. The closest we came to anything like that was crabs we got from supposedly a blanket from a friend. Later in our marriage HIV testing became a regular event.

I wonder how soon our children knew. I hate to think how much I damaged them in my waywardness. Much later in our marriage we confessed to them when they were adults about this time in our life. They both knew already; just not how bad it had gotten.

In my forties I accepted Jesus as my Lord and Savior. This life of sin had to end. It did, I thought. At that time, I was in a relationship. I told him we had to stop doing this because it was against God. However, we remained friends because our families were tied together. I hoped and prayed that he and his family would accept the Lord. But that was only another ruse. Even though we were not having sex, we were still talking. At a church conference, a message cut me so deep, I knew I had to cut this off for real. I confessed to some sisters about it. They told me this had to truly end, no more phone calls, no more e-mails, no more contact with anyone in his family – total and complete! Plus, I had to tell Dan about it!

"Dan, I need to tell you about Frank. For the past, several years we have been having an affair. It is over now because I no longer want to sin against God. I am soooo sorry." I could not look at him. It was the hardest thing I had to do.

"I figured you all were a couple. It will be ok," he answered solemnly. No rage or elevated voice. Dan is a still water that run deep; when he gets mad it comes out of nowhere. He was controlled and calm. I suspected he was having an affair. I hoped I was wrong.

Soon, I found myself attracted to a single brother in the church and it was mutual. We both fought it. There was never any sexual contact, but nonverbals and words were obvious. Thanks only to God, I was able to confess this attraction to several sisters who prayed with me, read the scriptures with me and advised me on my behavior. It was not easy relinquishing that desire for this brother, but with God, that battle was won. It amazes me now how I barely remember what I felt for that brother, especially if I happen to run into him at conferences.

With this new walk in life, I do not allow myself to be alone with any man, married or single. When a wife wants me to give her husband a ride, I seek out a sister who needs a ride, too. I cannot chance it. On the rare occasions I have had to be alone in a car because a brother needs a ride and no sister, I am praying endlessly until they get out and praising God for controlling the conversation. Anytime a brother wants to talk personally about something that as a woman, I should not know, I redirect him, "You need to talk to a brother about that." In my experience that is step one towards a more intimate relationship, talking about personal issues in life, especially if it is about their spouse or girlfriend. Quash it!

Songs or scriptures about the adulterous woman always bring tears to my eyes. Not tears of remorse or regret but tears of joy that God would love and save a woman like me. He watched and protected me all my life despite my turned back on him while I lay with other men. In spite of the hurt I gave to Dan, these other men and their wives, God still loved me. I should have been dead in the grave by jilted men and women. I should have been disease-ridden and dying from AIDs. I should have been beaten or raped. I should have experienced a lot more horrors, but God prevented them. He pulled me out of that grimy mess that I wallowed in, washed me clean and put on a crisp white robe. He continues to forgive me of my lack of compassion, negativity and other sins as they occur; His love never fails. I am eternally grateful for the plans He has for this forgiven woman.

In addition to being forgiven God has granted Dan and I many opportunities to forgive each other the hurts we inflected on one another. Hurts that took several years to heal. He also enabled us to reinstate trust. Trust was lost in our marriage, but through time and God's guidance trust was regained. Renewing our vows for our fortieth anniversary with family in a restaurant helped in that process.

Anytime I hear of couples who say they have over thirty years of marriage, I applaud and encourage them. I know they have a story to tell. Many years of marriage does not occur without the drama of being a couple. Family, finances, affairs, insecurities, and so on plague marriages. Despite all that, marriages like ours can thrive with God as we cling to Him.

CHAPTER FIVE

THE MOTHER

*"Can a mother forget the baby at her breast and
have no compassion on the child she has borne?
Though she may forget, I will not forget you!"*
Isaiah 49:15

I always wanted a large family. I thought I
was missing something by having only one
brother. I did not want to be a working mother; I
wanted to be home with our children. Dan and I
planned to have five children. However, after
Danny, Jr. popped into the world on November 30,
1975, I changed my mind. He came so fast that
the doctor had to catch him as he slid out with a
sloshy whoosh!

I loved being pregnant, even with morning
sickness; I loved the miracle of child development
in the womb. Delivering a baby, though painful,
was tolerable. I did not like the aftermath – raising
the child. Five children?! Oh no! Five personalities to deal with! Five kids to travel or not travel
with! I was spoiled from my parents. Five

children would have meant little or no traveling. I did not want that! Two would be good enough. It would take eight years before Tia arrived.

Dan's mom, Jackie, dreamed of fish anytime someone in the family was pregnant. She was always right! She dreamed of fish once between Danny Jr. and Tia. I was on birth control well into my second pregnancy – too far in! There was fear that the second child would be deformed because of the medication. Dan and I made the decision to have a "D and C" to terminate that pregnancy. There was no way we could bear life with a child that had a disability. I often wonder, if we had been in a better place in our relationship with God, would we have been able to have that second child. Ever since then, after the doctor termed our abortion as a "D and C," I often wondered when I heard my friends having this type of operation if it was really an abortion or a womb cleaning. Thanks to God, I have never had any regrets about that decision. Tia would not have existed if we had the second child.

In addition to a changed mind about five children over the two we had, I had to work. At first, I was not happy with the idea of working. To have the lifestyle that Dan and I wanted for our children I could not sit home. God must have laughed at my aspirations to stay home. A maternal instinct was not my strength. Escaping the whining, smelly diapers, crying and neediness of babies to go to work proved to be a blessing in disguise. Handing over our children to others more patient and attentive that myself was a relief. During periods of my husband's layoffs from work, I was more than glad to slip out of the house in the morning while he "watched" the baby. I never enjoyed working, but I did not want to be stuck at home either.

My mom worked; I worked. She breastfed; I breastfed. Bonding with our children through breastfeeding and giving them the best nourishment possible was important, even if I felt inadequate as a mom. Swollen with milk drippy breasts, and the occasional sharp bite was worth it to see the contentment in their faces, especially on sleepless nights for me.

"Mommy! Mommy! Play with me! Play with me!" I scribbled something on my paper from the book I was reading for one of my classes at Kent. "Mommy! Mommy!" A small hand pressed down hard on my book; it shut, nearly missing my fingers.

Glassy eyes peered at me. With a toy in hand and the other on the book, Dan, Jr. our first born with lip poked out stood there.

Arghhh! I thought, *I don't need this!* Frustration, anger and the urge to laugh at my son's cuteness tried to burst from my lips, so I bit them instead.

"I am sorry. What do you want to play?" Guilt overtook the other conflicting emotions. *How could I put my child before my studies? I have a test tomorrow and I need to study! Seriously, why am I in school anyway? This is way too hard.*

Attending school part-time, working full-time, being a mother and a wife was rarely easy. There was never enough time to do those roles and still have fun. Fun? Free time? What was that? Obtaining a baby sister was the hardest. Several times I had to take Dan. Jr. to class with me. I remember taking him to a Linguistics class; he was so attentive and interested in what the instructor was saying. I joked to my friends, "He is getting a college education early."

Once, I had to take him on a test day. As the "mindful" mother I packed him plenty of things to keep him occupied: crayons, coloring book, small toys he could play silently with and snacks. To keep his mouth busy I gave him a small colorful lifesaver. His smile of appreciation made me feel like the "good" mother that I was. I began my test eagerly hoping to get done quickly, so we could go home.

I heard a wee, "Cough! Cough!" I looked at my son with hands on his throat. I patted him a couple of times on the back. Then the sound of air sucking stopped the coughing, then silence, his lips turned blue. *What?* I thought. *He can't breathe?* I heard a gasp from someone. A flash of a story my husband told me about how one of his nieces or nephews who had a choking situation came. I stood up in the middle of a crowded classroom, with neat rows of classroom desks, and grabbed my child, turned him upside down and pounded several times on his back until the offending candy "pooshed" out of his mouth and rolled across the floor. "Waaaaah!" Tears drenched my son's cheeks. I stood there holding him and felt a thousand eyes piercing into my flesh. The whole class was looking at me in shock, disgust, indignation, and an assortment of other emotions. The air felt heavy; I struggled with catching my own breath. I tried to quietly put my son back in his seat, to finish the test.

"Juel, why don't you and your son come with me." It was the teacher. *Oh man, I was in trouble now.* He led us out like children going to the principal's office. He walked us down the hall, opened a door to a nearby room and led us in. "You can finish taking your test in this room."

I looked at him, with watery blurred vision and whispered, "Thank you."

I was so relieved, that was a final exam; I never had to see those classmates again. The next semester, I made sure I had a babysitter; otherwise, I did not go to class.

"I want a little sister, so I can read to her." Danny's ear pressed on my enlarged belly. His head popped up. "She kicked me!"

I had to laugh. "Maybe the baby wanted to get closer to you and had to move."

"I hope it is a girl."

"We will have to wait and see. It could be a boy."

"I want a sister!" he stomped.

We wanted a healthy girl also to have one of each. I do not know how "big brother" would have been if he had a little brother instead. Thank goodness, we did not have to find out. Tia was born, after several false labor pains, on September 23, 1983. Eight-year-old, Danny, was the hovering big brother. With eyes looking up at her big brother, Tia listened as he read all kinds of books to her. He was never apart from her, except when he had to go to school, or she was at the sitter's house.

When both were old enough, they attended preschool and before and after day care when in elementary. We did not want them in any institution while they were still in diapers; family or babysitters watched them instead. Every now and then, I felt guilty about working when babysitters proved to be unreliable sources of care or Danny and Tia cried about being left at a daycare center. That guilt was short lived; I had to work, especially when Dan was laid off. Being home alone with children was not a craving that wanted to be sated.

Raising two children eight years apart is like raising a single child, but two of them. There was rarely any sibling rivalry because they did not grow up in the same school or with the same circle of friends or felt the other got more attention. However, as I type this, I wonder.

It is said that fathers and daughters are closer, and mothers and sons are closer – something about being opposite sexes, a biological thing. That is true, with my own dad. I was closer to him than my mom. There was always some sort of tension between my mom and me. It grew stronger when I became a mom and we lived in the same house for the first year and a half of our marriage with an infant. As a mother, I could not do anything right, with my mother around telling me what to do when Danny cried. Moving to our own home helped me to make those first mother mistakes without my mom's watchful eye.

Danny, Jr. was a typical boy, an explorer, inquisitive and chatty. As he grew older, he became less chatty. For a period of time, he stuttered. He either grew out of it, learned to talk slower or got help from school. As an adult he remains quiet. He was the first to leave home for college. I considered myself close to him, but when he left for college that lack of mother instinct must have kicked in. I was eager for him to make his own way in the world. If I felt any kind of emotion, it was just from thinking of his coming of age and not being my little boy anymore, not tears of sadness because he would not be home. My husband, however, was choked up when we left him at Kent State.

Tia was my needy one, because of us. By the time she was born, Dan and I were fanatically involved in Boy Scouts. We were both Scout leaders of Cub, Boy and later Girl Scouts. We both trained leaders of Scouts and spent lots of time away from her and her brother. We got into Scouts for our children, but soon found ourselves not with them like we should have been.

"Mommy! Mommy! You are home! Guess what happened at school." With lips on fire she told me every detail and followed me around the house like a happy puppy. Every time we were together, she would be near me, with arms grabbing and holding me. I remember, pulling her off on a not-so-good day. I could not understand why she was so needy. I wish I knew then what I know now; she was looking for love from her mom. She even got baptized at church to please me. I did not know that then. Her neediness was not her fault. I often wondered, if I had given her the love she needed, would she have become a mother later in life, instead of when she was one month from being a seventeen-year-old.

The signs of her pregnancy were obvious. I can't remember if I asked her if she was pregnant or if something, I said made her confess. "Yes, I tried to get rid of it, but I was told I was too young and had to get permission from my parents." Rivers of tears, a baby coming into the house, a busy household, how was this going to work? Abortion or adoption was not an option in our household. I hope I told her it would be "OK". Sometime later I said, "I am not planning to raise your child. This is something you need to do. We are here for you for food and housing, but I will not be babysitting." I do not think I was harsh; I tried not to be. I did not have time to raise her child and do whatever I was doing. Plus, I did not want to be one of those grandmothers who raised the grandchildren while their child was out having a good time enjoying life without their children. I did not want her to have one child then another child, living on welfare.

"Girl, you are going to change your mind once that baby gets here!" Coworkers, friends, and church members told me repeatedly.

"Nope, that ain't happenin' here!" I shrugged. One friend, in particular, was doing that with her grandchildren. I thought, *I am not trying to be like you, with no life, because you are raising your grandchildren and your children are nowhere to be seen.*

"Bleep bleep!" The monitor showed contractions were in full intensity on the graph. Tia laughed while she talked, played cards and whatever else.

"Don't you feel that?" I asked.

"Nope, they gave me an Epidural. I don't feel a thing." She smiled and chatted with Patrick, her boyfriend and father of the baby. Her room was full of people – Patrick, Dan, me and Patrick's mom. Some of Tia's friends even popped in for a visit.

"Wow, I wish I had that when you and your brother were born. I had a spinal. They gave it to me too late. So, I felt everything, then was numb after you two were already here. Then threw it all up," I said and was amazed. She had to be told when it was time to push. With the full house of people, I wondered if she was going to let us all stay for the full labor. "These kids are so open with their lives, with dads at showers," I told my husband.

"You all can leave now," my daughter told us when it was time to push. I was relieved. I wanted her to have some privacy. I love watching birthing movies but did not want all these people watching my daughter. Patrick was the only one allowed to stay, as it should be. Kiara was born on August 19, 2000. She was given her father's last name.

Weeks before my grandchild's birth, my mom was admitted in the hospital again. For years she had been a renal dialysis patient, with other complications such as type 2 diabetes and other issues. She was bad. Dan and I admitted later thinking: "Mom is going out and the baby is coming in." It seemed like an exchange of life was about to happen. God had other plans. Mom saw her first great-grandchild before she died on December 24, 2000, five months later.

"It is OK, for you to stay home and mourn your mom," someone from church told me. Church service was on Christmas Eve; Mom died in the early morning of that same day.

"No, I can't. I NEED to be with the body right now." God had prepared me days before; I never thought it would be on Christmas Eve. The comfort of that service was best. Tears ran down my cheeks on a particular song about tomorrow not being promised. I looked up at the song leaders on the stage, all the women were crying with me as they sang. I placed the angel I had bought for my mother on my desk, never to be given, but remembered. I was happy she saw Kiara before she left her earthly body.

I cannot remember how Tia and Patrick managed to get babysitting for Kiara. Patrick's mom helped, but she also worked. Patrick was two years older than Tia; he loved her and wanted to marry her. We refused to give permission for her to marry while she was a minor. We told them once she turns eighteen if she wants to marry, then, so be it. Tia was a great mom and senior in High School. She worked hard even when the baby kept her up late nights. After graduation, she attended a local college.

"Aren't you and Patrick going to get married?" I asked one day. I just knew she was going to marry when she turned eighteen.

"No, I want to go to college first. Then we will marry." As a single independent mom, she found there were benefits. She was able to obtain public assistance, attend college for free, received vouchered day care, baby furniture, clothes, diapers and other things needed to raise a baby. She lived in our home as a nondependent. We had to take her off our income tax return.

I hated to think this, but her pregnancy was a blessing. We did not have to take on student loans like we did with our son. Saving money for college was not easy for us; there was never enough to save to live on, let alone for college. We enjoyed the benefits of having our daughter and granddaughter close by without the financial strain. We helped with household expenses and with care while they were home, but babysitting was a rarity.

Tia worked and went to school. When Kiara was six, Tia and Patrick decided to marry. She was not quite finished with school, but they didn't want to wait any longer. Besides, they wanted to live in their own home. I understood that; I could not wait to get out of my parents' house. All these years, Tia lived in our house with Kiara and Patrick lived with his mom. Kiara was six years old going on seven when she walked down the aisle in her flower girl dress for her parents.

Thirteen years later, Kiara welcomed her little brother, Patrick, Jr. to the family. She was so protective of him. "Grandma, PJ doesn't like it when you do this and that, he likes it this way." She was always telling me how wrong I was caring for him.

"Girl, I raised your momma and you, I know what he needs!" As a grandmother for the second time, with this child, I had the most involvement. I was at a place I could help – retired. I was still active in whatever, but I was compelled to be the grandmother I could not be for Kiara. Spending three to five days a week with PJ was included in my schedule, while his parents worked. Where I was, so was PJ.

Danny, Jr. and Tia are now both adults – forty-four and thirty-six years old, respectively. How is that possible? Despite how I played a part in damaging them through their young years, they are both productive members in society with jobs. Danny, Jr. is single, living in Maryland, working for the State in a private office with a window. Tia works in the medical field at a hospital; she and Patrick have thirteen years of marriage. Kiara graduated from High School in June 2018 and attends college at Cuyahoga Community College. Patrick, Jr. is six and in kindergarten.

Thanks only to God, our children are the mature adults they are in spite of their mom.

CHAPTER SIX

THE BOY SCOUT AND *GIRL SCOUT LEADER*

"Fathers, do not exasperate your children; instead bring them up in the training and instruction of the Lord." Ephesians 6:4.

"It only takes an hour a week! We need parents to be involved as den leaders for the Pack," said the tall man in a tan uniform with blue epaulets with assorted pins and patches on his arms and chest. The stillness hurt the ears.

I rubbed my swollen belly with my left hand; my right hand shot up. "I will be a den leader." Eyes of disbelief looked at me. I was due any time and I wanted my son, Danny to be in the Cub Scouts.

Clinton, the Cubmaster, smiled at me, "No, you don't have to, you are having a baby soon." But he eventually accepted my offer and soon several other hands rose.

I am always the reluctant leader. I led because no one else wanted to. Danny, Jr. was in the first grade and ready to be a Tiger Cub Scout. My husband was encouraged to be Assistant Scoutmaster, but soon became Scoutmaster of Boy Scout Troop 464. The Cub Scout Pack 464 and Boy Scout Troop 464 were units sponsored by Eastside Christian Reformed Church in Warrensville Heights, Ohio. My husband had a long history of being a Boy Scout as a child and was eager for his son to have that same experience. I had been a Girl Scout, but all our troop did was meet and have milk and cookies. I grew bored of that and quit; I wanted more. Since my husband was occupied with the older Boy Scouts, he could not do both Cub Scouts and Boy Scouts. I was hoping to be like most parents, drop Danny off and let someone else develop him as a scout. But, when I saw no one else wanted to help, I rose my hand.

Therefore, Tia, my second child, was born into Scouting. She was with me for Cub Scout den meetings, pack meetings, and as she grew older, she was involved in Boy Scout events.

"I am going to be a Boy Scout when I get old enough," she squealed, as she bounced around in the grass.

"No, honey, you will be a Girl Scout when you get old enough." Her head cocked and looked at me with wonder.

Our den meetings were held in our small bungalow on Hickory Lane. After Tiger Cubs I moved up with the small group of four to eight boys into Wolf Cubs and Bear Cubs. When they became Webelos Scouts a male leader had them as they transitioned into becoming Boy Scouts. I loved all the activities we did with them in the home and in nature to help them earn the various badge levels and to encourage them to think for themselves. Even with Tia crawling around, it was fun.

Dan and I were intensely involved in the Cub and Boy Scout Troop as parents and leaders. The years flew, and our schedule became all about Scouting. It seemed like every week we were in meetings, camping, activities, leaders' meetings – anything that had to do with Scouting. Tia was dragged to many of those places.

When she turned five, we joined the Girl Scouts. I felt since I had spent five years as a Cub and Boy Scout Leader, I would do the same for her. I went to training to be a Girl Scout leader before she was eligible to be in a troop. Therefore, Tia and I joined as Daisy Scout and Leader in Troop 282. Now our world was complete – Cub, Boy and Girl Scouts.

We wanted them to experience the outdoor world and become outstanding citizens in our community from what could be gained through these organizations. Hopefully, they both can say that now as adults that is what happened. However, I know they both can say they also lost their parents along the way.

Soon we found ourselves in leadership roles that took us away from home and our children. We both were leaders on the District Level where we oversaw other troops and packs and assisted them with the leadership. We both taught new Cub, and new Boy Scout leaders how to manage their units. I took it a step further and trained Girl Scout leaders to do the same with their units. We both attended advanced Boy Scout training called Woodbadge and earned our Woodbadge Beads. I also went to Cub Woodbadge and earned Wood-badge beads for those. Eventually, we both taught those advance Woodbadge courses, he in Boy Scouts, me in Cub Scouts. We also were members of the Order of the Arrow as Boy Scout Leaders. We received all kinds of awards from our "sacri-fice." One of the top awards was the Silver Beaver. We were fanatics and loved it.

As a family, we drove out to Philmont Scout Ranch in New Mexico. Our son took part with a group who hiked the range. We were there for a week; we never saw him while he was camping and hiking the range. Our daughter was in a group of her peers while they did arts and crafts and whatever to keep them occupied. She was four years old. While she was with her group, Dan and I attended classes that related to the current lead-ership role we were in. Philmont was for training leaders to be the best they could be, along with their children. We dined every night with Tia and spent the rest of the evening together. The three of us stayed in a canvas tent on wooden platforms. They were electrified; it was like having luxuries while being in the out of doors. We slept on cots with medal frames and mattresses.

While we were out there, somehow, our names, as a couple, were submitted for a special honor. We were selected to be featured in *"Scouting Magazine."* This interview came later when we were back home. A photographer and reporter came out to the house. Pictures of us were taken in various scenic spots in Cleveland. They attended a training session we both were involved in and took pictures of us leading that group. They took pictures of our interaction with our children. We laugh to this day about the picture of Dan and Dan, Jr. playing basketball, like they did this all the time. The story came out in the September 1989, *"Scouting Magazine."* We were instant celebs on the Scouting front. This validated what we were doing for the community.

Our children suffered. They did not get the attention they should have when they were young from us. Yes, they gained a world of experiences. Our son went to Jamborees and other Scout adventures without us. Our daughter traveled to Northern Michigan, Texas and the United Kingdom with Girl Scout travel groups and flew on her own to these places as an escorted minor. One trip she was old enough not to be escorted. Her first connection missed the second connection and somehow on her own she was able to get herself on another plane home. Many of these journeys for them could not have been had if it were not for Scouting. I often wonder how their lives might have been different if we had been there when they needed us as teenagers while we were out with other adults in the name of Scouting.

Scouting was our god! Other distractions, people, family and activities came in second or not

at all because of Scouting. My husband's nick-
name at work was "The Boy Scout." Not just
because he was involved, because of his behavior.
He always saw the good in everything. Even when
he got mad. He did not always act as the others
did in volatile situations. Our plan was to sign up
as lifetime Scout Leaders for our grandchildren,
but it never got that far.

The world around us changed. The children
we served changed. The parents changed. Other
opportunities pulled at the troop and future scouts;
many chose those things over Scouting. Parent
participation was rarely there, but even that grew
less and less and sometimes combative.

As my Girl Scout troop increased, I weaned
myself off Boy Scout and Girl Scout teaching. I
was learning to let some of the roles go. It was fun
but draining. I learned to say "no." I also saw how
my daughter needed me more, yet I wanted to finish my Girl Scouting days with her on the troop
level only. My husband, also, weaned off district
and council level positions and stayed on the troop
level for several years after our son completed
Scouts. Thoughts of lifetime leadership waned for
us. Years later, with lack of parent support and
disinterested scouts, Dan said goodbye to Scouting. With no new leadership to take over the
troop, Troop 464 closed its doors.

I was with our Troop 282 from Daisy Scouts
until Senior Scouts. We did so much together!
Sharing the journey with these girls from five
years old until their high school years was full.
We traveled by plane, train, and car to various

places. They earned badges, helped in the community, grew and became leaders. Very few of them were ashamed to say they were Girl Scouts. They wore their uniforms with pride in Memorial Day parades. We camped, went wild caving in Kentucky and more. We even had a huge Girl Scout Troop 282 website, with multiple links to help other troops. It was a well visited website by troops all over the world.

We even were involved in an Amtrak derailment on our way to Savannah, Georgia. As we approached our last stop before Savannah, we were ready to get off this long train ride. Then we felt a jerk like someone had stepped on the brakes hard. Our heads flew forward and back. Suddenly our car leaned to the right and back to the left repeatedly. I could see through to the other car in front of us and it was leaning back and forth like ours but in the opposite direction; when our car leaned left the other car leaned right, back and forth, tossing us side to side. We learned later that a lowboy tracker trailer truck had gotten stuck on the track and the Amtrak train leaped over and through the truck.

We are derailing! I thought. Thoughts of another derailment in the news when people fell into the alligator infested swamps filled my head. We were in the south and that thought gripped my heart. *God don't let anyone in our group be hurt.* I got a sense of peace that no one would.

None of us were injured. When the media found out we were a Girl Scout troop on the train they interviewed us and showed it on TV. This was before cell phones, so we were unable to call our families back home to assure them we were unharmed. It took a while to contact them after we were transported to a safe place. When I called the families, none of them had a clue. Our city was in the middle of the World Series and the Cleveland Indians were in the limelight. Their eyes were focused on that. Since there were no fatalities, it did not make national news as a big headliner, just the local areas.

In Savannah, our troop got the royal treatment from the local Girl Scout Council. We were there to visit the Juliette Gordon Low birthplace, the founder of Girl Scouts. Despite all the fun we were having, it became apparent that the girls were fearing the ride back on the train. Only one girl could afford a one-way plane ride at the last moment; the rest of us would have to take the train. The more they talked about the return, the more I realized we all needed the counseling that was offered by Amtrak. We all spilled our guts about the emotions that had transpired in this accident in counseling. It helped but did not solve our transportation concerns. Somehow our local Lake Erie Girl Council heard about this dilemma. They offered and paid for a one-way flight back home for all of us. A sigh of relief engulfed us, and we were able to completely enjoy the rest of our trip. The troop purchased a special Juliette Gordon Low framed picture that we all signed with our thanks. We presented this thank you gift to the council after we returned home.

"Let's decide a date for our next Bible study," One of the ladies said. We all opened our calendars. "How about the sixth?"

"I have a Scout meeting," I said.

"The eighth?"

"Oh, no that is a Scout leader's meeting."

"The tenth?"

"Campout. Sorry."

"Hold up!" Two of us were studying the Bible with a woman who chirped in. "You just told me in the scriptures about denying myself, yet you can't find time in *your* schedule to study with me."

Gasp! "Oh, my goodness. I am soooo sorry; this is not right. I won't go to that leader's meeting. Let's do it then." I felt like a hypocrite.

That was God's way of telling me, my Scouting days were over. Weaning myself off a few Scouting obligations was not enough. He wanted me to cut it off completely. I did not want to do it but knew it was something God needed me to do in this walk with Him.

By then, Tia had earned her Gold Award and others were thinking about doing the same. The timing was right and yet not so right. Most of them were in 11th grade and we had a year or so left as Scouts.

"No, Mrs. Fitz! This is not fair! Why do you have to do this?" A chorus of girls wailed.

"I must; God needs me to do something else." No matter what I said, it was not acceptable.

We were unable to get another parent to take over the leadership role. After a closing time together, the troop folded. How often, I wish I could have waited another year. I am so grateful that there is still a closeness with these girls. They are now all adults, with children, husbands and jobs. All of them are leaders of some sort in their life. They are all independent as married or single women. I thank God, for Girl Scouts gave them those skills to be productive members in their communities.

Even though Scouting became our idol, it gave us something in common to do as a couple, matured our children, exposed our family to worlds we could only imagine, and gave us long-lasting friendships.

Through Scouting my eyes were opened. I was able to put aside this idol that had great community worth but separated me from God. By removing this, I grew closer to God.

CHAPTER SEVEN

THE IRS AGENT

*"Slaves, obey your earthly masters with respect
and fear, and with sincerity of heart, just as you
would obey Christ. Obey them not only to win
their favor when their eye is on you, but as slaves
of Christ, doing the will of God from your
heart. Serve wholeheartedly, as if you were serving the Lord, not people, because you know that
the Lord will reward each one for whatever good
they do, whether they are slave or free." Ephesians 6:5-8.*

My parents were government employees: so,
I became one.

"Take vocational courses to get your foot in
the door and use the college prep to advance you,"
both of my parents told me.

In high school I was encouraged to take ste-
nography courses and college preparation classes.
It was a tight schedule which required me to take
three years of summer school classes. My parents
also enrolled me in activities to keep me out of

trouble. It turned out to be the best thing they led me to do.

My first jobs with the government were all clerical or stenographical in nature, file clerks, diet clerk and clerk typist. At Navy Finance Center, Veterans Administration Hospital and the Internal Revenue Service, I filed and typed my daytime hours for pay. I worked at Navy Finance for the first summer after graduating from high school as a clerk typist. At the VA, I worked for a year as a diet clerk. Both were full-time positions that I resigned from for better things.

I transferred to the Internal Revenue Service from the VA to be a file clerk for a position termed as "temporary not to exceed ninety days." My hope was that it would turn into a permanent position. I was not quite happy at the VA and was ready for a change. I filed as a Grade 2 employee for small bucks, but it was a lot in my eyes at the time. As hoped, I was asked to stay for another ninety days, temporarily. After or before that second stay, my memory fails me, I was off for a few months and was able to live on unemployment. Then, I was called back for another temporary ninety days as a clerk typist in the same area I did all the filing in. They liked my work and soon I was able to gain a position as a full-time clerk typist in a typing pool. I loved having my own desk and typing the assignments they gave me. We were in a large room with twenty or so other typist and no partitions.

I worked in the Federal Building in downtown Cleveland and took the Rapid Transit, our city's, train system into town, and the bus. I took the bus to the train and made a transfer to the train into town. It took maybe an hour, but it gave me the golden chance to read or sleep. If I slept, I always had a fear of missing my stop. It did happen once. I woke up at end of the line and had to take the train back to my stop – that was a good sleep.

"Girl, if you are going to advance in this organization, you need to take some Accounting," my best friend in the typing pool said. She was old enough to be my mother and she treated me like her daughter. *Accounting? Why do I want to take Accounting? I am not into numbers; I like to write.* However, I took her advice and enrolled at Cuyahoga Community College for Accounting.

Several years had passed in this typing pool. I had applied for various positions in the organization but was never accepted. I also kept my name on the Civil Service list for other positions in other organizations, just in case. One day I got a notice in the mail for a full-time stenographer position at the IRS. I called and was scheduled for an interview.

"I was surprised to see you already work here at the IRS. I got your name from the Civil Service roster. Why didn't you apply from within?" Bob the interviewer asked.

"I have applied for several positions and either haven't been accepted or haven't heard anything back from them. So, I kept my name on the list just in case other positions in other agencies come up."

"I am glad you did, there was nothing in our records about your application. I thought there were no applicants. So, I had to go to the list for eligible people."

That was the interview that allowed me to move from the typist pool to be a stenographer for Bob who managed a group of revenue agents. I had my own desk outside of his office. I loved having a full desk where I placed family pictures and other personal items. Answering phones, timekeeping, typing reports, taking shorthand, typing memorandums and other duties for him and the agents in the group was a thrill for me. It felt good to be of service to so many. When it was learned that I got the position, there was a shock wave in the typing pool. All of us had tried to get out; I was able to escape. Thanks to a wise person who told me to keep my name on the Civil Service register I was able to move out of the typing pool.

I loved this job as stenographer; but I continued to take classes in accounting. This was my favorite job in the organization. Interacting with the revenue agents and my boss was never boring; it was different every day. When the agents were in the office, they sat in an open area with large hip to ceiling windows on three of the walls with two agents at a table with papers spread out as they did their examinations of various taxpayers. Most of the time they were in the field doing their exams at the taxpayer's place of business or in the taxpayers' homes. My daily contact was with Bob as he managed from his office.

"You were such a quiet little mouse when I hired you; I took you and made you into something great!" he always reminds me when I see him decades later at retirement parties. He encouraged me to continue in my Accounting studies and helped me when I had questions. He especially directed me to attend Toastmasters.

Attending Toastmasters every week was the best advice I have ever gotten. It taught me how to speak in public, something I love to do. Speaking from a stage is so much easier for me to do than one-on-one conversations with people. If I know my material, speaking in front of lots of people is fun. I like to be the speaker/teacher that keeps a person like me awake, not like the speaker that puts me to sleep. Sitting for long periods of time listening to someone speak, make my eyelids fall. But speakers who are lively, interactive and interesting, keep me awake. While I was a stenographer, I had no idea how Toastmasters would help me later in life.

Several years passed and I thought about how I would love staying in this position; it was so much fun. But God knows nothing lasts forever; there is always a time to move on to other things. With several Accounting courses under my belt I applied to be a Tax Auditor and was accepted.

Tax auditors stay in the office. I had my own soft, orange-clothed cubicle and desk. The room was filed with several of these cubicles of other auditors. A low murmur of sound filled the air with an occasional loud cry of despair or anger. We all tried not to listen, but our itchy ears always perked up. Every day I saw three to four taxpayers in my cube. As a tax auditor we examined the 1040's of people. I learned to read documents upside down before the person gave them to me. I learned to read people's nonverbals to see if their story was true. It was an interesting job. It was a definite pay increase, but it was not always enjoyable.

"Why? Why? I pay everything for them! If it weren't for me, they would have no place to stay. Are you saying I need to kick them out?" the woman sobbed at my desk.

"No, I am not saying that. I am saying because they get welfare, the public assistance is paying more than half of their support. In order for you to claim them as a deduction, you have to show you paid over half of their support. So, we must disallow your deduction for them as an exemption," I explained. My explanation was never a comfort. I did not like making people who had no money pay more.

Being a tax auditor was hard work! We had to have so many audits done in a day and we did not get much time to review the file before the taxpayer came in.

"We need someone to be the steward Jack retired, and the space is open." No one wanted this job. As a reluctant leader, I volunteered for this. I must have lost my mind. I hate confrontation, but I took on the role anyway. Of course, I was told, we don't have problems in the position I had. I soon learned that was not true. We did. I will never forget losing one battle for one grievant.

She had been passed over for promotions and felt wronged. It took her years to stop being mad at me for how that situation went down.

Soon with more Accounting classes completed, I applied and was accepted to be an Internal Revenue Agent, another promotion. I was happy to escape the sobs of taxpayers to examine small businesses and corporations. Plus, it released me from being a steward.

Interviewing taxpayers and seeing the various places of business was the fun part of the examination. I was amazed at the types of businesses there were out there and what people did for a living. The funeral home is an obvious business, but who thinks about how bodies are transported from various cities when people die away from home. For any examination it was always important to speak with taxpayers and take a tour of the company. I loved seeing behind-the-scenes of businesses.

The worst part is I could not talk about my job to anyone. So, my husband, family or friends never knew where I was. I rarely told people what I did. "I work for the Treasury Department," I would tell people who asked. At one point in time we were told it is not wise to tell people we work for the IRS because there were people who did not like us and might try to harm us. Years down the road, when I became a part-time travel agent, it was easy to not talk about working full-time with IRS and say I was a travel agent.

"You are a double agent," my dad said.

"Double agent? What are you talking about?!" I was offended that he would think I was being two faced about something or a traitor.

"You are! You are an IRS Agent and a Travel Agent." He laughed loudly.

"Oh," I paused. "I guess you are right. I am a double agent. I accept that." I joined him in laughter.

It was like having a family at IRS. We worked at our jobs during the day, but we also spent lots of time in the evening and weekends together. We had parties, went to bars and played games like volleyball, flag football, baseball, bowling and other sports. I loved bowling and the flag football. "I got the flag!" I would wave the flag in the air grinning as the runner standing in the end zone sulked. Rushing the quarterback was my favorite thing to do. One of these moves brought a foot to my face. Thank goodness there were no cleats allowed. With several stitches in my face, I was back in the game a few weeks later.

The rough part about being an agent was the examination. After the interview, the work began. Reviewing countless documents, accounting systems, asking questions, watching nonverbals, calculations and preparing adjustment reports filled my days. Sometimes I wondered if I missed something when I gave refunds or found no adjustments.

"You are definitely not what I expected," one taxpayer said.

"What were you expecting?"

"I thought you were going to be this beady-eyed man, who was going to give me a hard time. You are quite pleasant, even though you are telling me I owe taxes." I heard that a lot.

As an agent I moved to various offices in order to be upwardly mobile. I worked in the downtown Cleveland Federal Building, Akron Federal Building, Bedford Heights and Independence.

Eventually I moved up in the organization to be an IRS Agent that examined the Fortune 500 size corporation. These examinations were done as a team of specialists. For two to three years, as a team, we would exam their corporate returns. The corporation provided office space where we viewed their books, records and invoices, interviewed people, took tours, traveled to other offices out of town, whatever was needed to complete the examination. We all had specific assignments to examine as part of the team.

It was always rough running into someone I know at one of these corporations and not reveal why I was there without lying. "I can neither confirm nor deny." was a part of our standard answer when asked a direct question of what I was doing during the day. The few who knew I worked for the IRS had to figure it out on their own.

As an agent during these years it was just a job for me. I was not out to find fault, just the truth. I was not one of the best. I hoped people were honest and that I did not have to tell them they owed money. Yet, if they were fraudulent, they deserved whatever was coming to them. I enjoyed educating people about what should have happened. I also felt like I was on the wrong side of the table – looking for fault instead of teaching them what they should do. When opportunities came for me to teach, I jumped on it.

Teaching the public to prepare tax returns in the community for free was exciting. I did not want to prepare returns, but taught others do it for those in need. I hated preparing my own return. Why would I want to prepare someone else's return?

Traveling to teach new Tax Auditors and IRS Agents to do their jobs was what I enjoyed most. Creating flip charts, power points, outlines and motivating people to learn made me happy.

"And the winners are: Mark, Bob and Juel for Hawaii!" My eyes bucked. Three of us had our names pulled from a hat to teach the new software system to revenue agents in Hawaii! Alaska was another choice that three others got chosen for. This was handled in the most unorthodox way. Normally, people who are closest to a destination for economic reasons are selected to go. I knew Californians would get the Hawaii and Alaska gigs. But no, a lottery was done, and I won Hawaii! Traveling on the government dime helped me in my 50-state quest. My dad and brother traveled with me on this trip. While I worked, they played all day.

"No need to dress up here. Don't make it obvious you are a main lander." I was happy to discard the profession dress while I worked in Honolulu.

It was not all work. In the evenings I enjoyed the 80-degree temperatures while it was cold in November at home. I also flew out several days before my assignment. I spent time in the home of a fellow sister from the church. The first morning, since my body was five hours ahead of Hawaii, Chenise took me out to watch the sunrise. I even got the chance to serve on a special HOPE *worldwide* project at an elementary school before checking into my hotel. My father and brother arrived after I checked into the hotel. They had spent several days with family in Los Angeles. They left a few days before I finished my stay there. After the trip, before getting on my plane, I went on a guided hike to see one of their waterfalls.

This was in 2001, two months after the towers fell in New York City. Flying by plane was intense. The government had scheduled four one-way flights – two out and two back on different airlines. Since it looked like I was taking one-way stops I was searched deeply on each flight. I learned what it felt like to be profiled.

The government sent me to several other states that helped me with my 50-state quest. That quest was achieved in 2014, three years after retirement. However, if it were not for the trips at the IRS it would have taken longer.

Somewhere in time, I longed to be free of the IRS. I hoped that my entrepreneur ventures with Prepaid Legal, Premier Jewelry and ownership of Juel's Travel and Cruises would replace my government income; none of these ever did – merely additional income. I continued to work, hope and enjoy breaks through teaching and training assignments.

Maybe three to five years before retirement, God gave me a new job in the organization – Tax Computation Specialist. No longer did I go out in the field to examine taxpayers and make adjustments to their tax returns. In my cubicle I prepared the income tax adjustment reports that field agents made for taxpayers. They no longer had to do these reports; a pool of Tax Computation Specialists did it for them. They did the audits, while we did their adjustment reports. I *loved* this! I loved it so much I was tempted to change my retirement date from April 1, 2011 to some later date. "No, Juel; your date is April 1, 2011," the Holy Spirit told me.

In addition to that, I was a specialist who assisted agents with one of our software programs. When they had a problem with the program, they called me, and I helped them through it. I loved both positions – serving others to do their jobs. Because God softened my heart and injected thankfulness in me for having a job, I was rewarded with work I enjoyed and left IRS on a high note instead of a negative one.

With thirty-seven years of government employment at three agencies, God enabled me to be promoted from a Grade 2, File Clerk, to a Grade 13, Tax Computation Specialist. By sticking it out with God, I get to enjoy a decent pension while I have breath in my body. Getting that foot in the door with vocational experience along with college high school preparation classes and college courses was key in my advancement. God's gift of parents who steered me in the right direction helped me to be the best I could be in the work force.

Looking back now, makes me smile for all the good times that dim the memories of the bad times, that turned out to be for my best.

CHAPTER EIGHT

THE TRAVEL AGENT

"We know that we have come to know him if we obey his commands. The man who says, 'I know him,' but does not do what he commands is a liar, and the truth is not in him. But if anyone obeys his word, God's love is truly made complete in him." I John 2:3-5b.

It is my parents' fault that I love to travel. We drove everywhere – to the east coast, to the west coast, to the Deep South and crossed the border into Canada. If it had been safer, we probably would have driven south into Mexico. However, I did do that later as an adult. No less than every quarter, we were in the car for a long weekend or for a week or two. Since they were government employees getting off from work was easy.

Traveling for me is an addiction! If I am not going somewhere every quarter, I like to say I start to have a tick in my flesh. Something calls me to leave my home to see faraway places. My hand was always up first when my employer needed volunteers to teach or be trained out of town – "send me."

During a dry travel spell, a relative died. *Wooo whoo* I thought, *I am on the road again.* I was so happy to be traveling anywhere, even if it meant going to a funeral. "On the Road Again" by Willie Nelson is one of my favorite travel songs.

As a Girl Scout and Boy Scout leader I loved helping make group arrangements for our troops. This happened so often, I began to think I should make a career of this. I saw an ad in the local Sunday newspaper, "*The Plain Dealer*" asking for interested people who wanted to be trained as a Cruise Specialist. I jumped on it. My training was through Premier Travel with whom I became a travel agent. It was an exciting course which included inspection of cruise ships in dock. I worked for them from 1996 until 1998.

My sister-in-law, Gayle, was a travel agent with Colony Crossings Travel in Tampa. She convinced me to join that agency. I worked for them for two years while I lived in Cleveland. The long-distance relationship with the agency sometimes was difficult because we sold from two different environments and what applied in Florida did not apply in Ohio. On a Carnival Cruise Line Familiarization trip in Miami, I met the owner of Cruisewiz from my local area.

"You need to come work with me in Cleveland," she said. "Working with me in the

Cleveland area will benefit you." So, I did. Training was my focus with Cruisewiz.

During the three years with Cruisewiz I became a Certified Travel Agent with the Institute of Certified Travel Agents in 2001. I earned the rank of Accredited Cruise Counsellor with the Cruise Lines International Association on March 2003.

For some reason or another, God led me to join Travel Planners as an Independent Travel Agent as scary thoughts of owning my own travel agency danced in my head. From March 2003 to March 2004 I gained more knowledge through Travel Planners and became a Master Cruise Counsellor with the Cruise Lines International Association in February 2004.

"Is that what you want me to do, God?" I prayed. "Having my own agency has its rewards – 100 percent commission! I would not have to share my commission! But, it's a lot of work! I must develop relationships with a lot of different vendors. I am a nobody now with them and they will pay me the lowest commission because of that. Then there is the liability, company name and so on. Plus, I am still working full time with the IRS." Despite these hesitations on March 21, 2004, Juel's Travel and Cruises was born.

Working with and training two to five travel agents within the company was fun and profitable; however, it was work. I learned what it meant to be on call 24/7. There were several times I took off from IRS on annual leave because of business that had to be dealt with in the agency. I kept praying that this agency would release me from IRS.

"What? You missed your flight?" I asked a new wife-to-be who called me while I was on vacation in Virginia. This couple was flying to another country to be married with family and friends. I jumped out of bed and made all the new arrangements to get them there and to push back the wedding ceremony. They had to leave the next day. The next morning, I called, "Just calling to make sure you are up." She laughed, "We are. We set several clocks to make sure we didn't miss the flight this time." I learned to carry my computer with me everywhere on my vacation in case something like that happened again. I did not like being on call 24/7, but it was the nature of the beast; stuff happens.

The hand of the reluctant leader flew up from my shoulder again; I became the Outside Sales Support Network Chapter Director for independent travel agents in the Cleveland area in June 2004. I must have had a passion to fill up every second of my time with stuff to do – crazy! Every month I had to arrange for a supplier from one of our travel partners to come to a monthly meeting for local agents to tell us about their companies so that we would be compelled to sell their product. Sometimes I would do some sort of training. It varied.

Several years in as an owner, I heard God say, "it's time for you to let this go."

"What are you talking about? I *love* travel; it is what I do. It is the talent *you* gave me! It is what I am hoping to leave IRS for! Ok, I *am* doing too much. So maybe you are telling me to stop doing whatever else I am doing – you can't mean travel."

"It's time to give this up!"

"No, no! Not yet!"

One year, I was thrilled about the commission I was going to get for the largest group I had ever had. As the days to the trip drew close and the monies were coming in from the group to pay the supplier, I noticed something was not quite right. I had forgotten to add a vital piece in their travel arrangements and had not charged the group for it. It meant I *owed* the supplier money and would not be getting a dime of commission. How did I do that? Was I so busy doing whatever that I lost focus on this account? I do not know. I was going to have a loss. I threw my hands ups. "I give, God! I am done! I should have let this go, two years ago like you told me to." Somehow, after talking with the supplier, God enabled me to have a small profit and not owe the supplier. I still cannot tell you how that happened. God's math is amazing!

When I made the decision to give up the travel agency in 2007, it was like a huge weight had been lifted off my shoulders. I was free! I was giddy about leaving the thing I love – helping others to travel. It was not about the money; I love to travel, and I love to help others do the same.

From 2007 until September 2014 God placed me in various forms of service that have nothing to do with travel. However, my husband and I continued to travel personally and included others with us. All during those years, I kept saying, "I wish I knew about that when I was a travel agent" or "I wish had use of this new technology as a travel agent." God blessed my husband and I by allowing us to complete our 50-state quest in August 2014. What an adventure that was to see all fifty states in our lifetime!

Then in the summer of 2014 as I was planning two group cruises for my husband and friends (an Alaskan cruise and a Disney cruise), I heard God say, "treat these cruises as you would as a travel agent." I had booked them under my girlfriend's travel agency, like I would have as one of her agents, but wasn't. I wanted her to get the commission.

Vivian of Viviano's Cruises and Tours had been stalking me since I closed the company and when I was an owner; she wanted me to work with her. She turned up the heat when the business folded.

"No, no, no! God told me I was out, and I can't go against that! I will just book my own travel under you. I am good."

Then I heard again, "treat these cruises as you would as a travel agent." To me that meant putting gifts in their cabins, decorating their cabins, and an assortment of other things I did as a travel agent. I shrugged my shoulders and wondered what that was about. Why would the Holy Spirit tell me to do that? I did it for both cruises and thought no more about.

September 2014 after both cruises were complete with fun memories galore for all, "I want you back in the travel industry, but with Vivian."

"Huh?"

"I want you back as a travel agent with Vivian."

"No way! For real? As a travel agent? Really?"

I teased Vivian, "Your stalking paid off, now we get to work together as travel agents in your company." We were both thrilled.

"Now we are partners," she told me and has continued to remind me years later.

I discovered the seven years out of the travel industry was God's training ground for me. He placed me in areas that I might not have been part of if I were running a company. During this time, I lost weight at Weight Watchers and became a Weight Watchers leader. I traveled, learned the new technology and the usefulness of social media for business. Many new relationships were developed during this time. Also, during those years, I retired from the Internal Revenue Service and graduated from Kent State University. Seven years of change, growth and renewal. So, in the year of perfection, God called me back to the service I loved – helping others make their travel dreams come true.

This second chance in the industry has been different. My attitude with God was: "You want me to do what, see who, go where, learn what – I am there!" No more doing it my way. No more spending tons of money on advertising. Use of social media, travel and spiritual devotional blogs and the word of God's service through me spread. Paying customers came out of nowhere. I loved not having the responsibility of being the boss. It is so much more fun and less stressful being a travel agent than the owner. It is unknown how long God wants me to be in this role, but while I am here, I will do whatever he needs me to do in the time he grants me. It's not often in business someone gets a second chance to do it God's way. Now, when God tells me to go here, speak to this person, take a course, do this or do not do that, I act immediately. Before I either did not hear Him or questioned what he told me. Being obedient to His call and commands are more important than doing it my way.

This was supposed to be the end of this chapter; but wait, there is more! On February 27, 2020, God made it clear that my days as a travel agent were ending. It has been five-and-a-half years since God allowed me back in the travel industry. These were my best years financially, even though I had to share my commission. If a passion becomes a job, it is time to leave. I was not in the travel business solely to make money. I simply loved helping others benefit from my travel obsession. The money was a bonus. The funds gained through travel were not enough to use as the foundation for a budget. Commissions came generally after travel was done. When the checks came, they were always right on time. Yet when I sat down to determine my ratio of effort invested to the amount I had earned, most times the hourly rate was minimal. I often entertained the thought, "Is this really worth it?"

During February 2020, God added new responsibilities to my schedule. He gave me a wonderful part time job at Chick-fil-A® and placed me on the church's board to replace an outgoing member. After two paychecks, I realized I was making more per hour being God's servant at a restaurant than as a travel agent – funds upon which I could legitimately base a budget. Both endeavors took time away from being a travel agent.

Oddly, I was not saddened by this change God wanted me to make. This time it is more of a pleasure to follow God's lead concerning His ultimate destination for me. I do not know where that will be, but I know it will be for my good. COVID-19 also sealed the deal for me. It is obvious major changes in travel will occur in the future and God does not want me to be part of the new world of travel as an agent. Traveling will always be a passion for me; but the era of selling those services has ended.

CHAPTER NINE

THE WRITER

" 'This is what the Lord, the God of Israel, says: 'Write in a book all the words I have spoken to you.' '" Jeremiah 30:2

"Write it now!"

"I don't have time. I have to get to work."

"Write it now!"

"Why would I want to tell people about that?"

"Write it now!"

"Gotta go, running late for work!" I jumped in my car and sped to work. All day long, "Write it now!" nagged at me. I could barely concentrate on what I had to do because of heavy pressure on my mind. The day dragged; I could not wait to get home.

I sped home, sat at my computer and typed out what was heavy on my heart. After proofreading and editing it, I put it in an e-mail and sent it to everyone on my distribution list.

Whoosh! Something pushed out of me and I sat, drained at peace, done. *What the heck was that all about?*

A new e-mail response appeared on my screen for the missive I had sent. *Oh man, what is this all about?* I thought, ready for a fight.

"Girl, that came right on time. I have been praying about that very issue all day and bam you write about it! Thanks for sending it!"

I sighed. "Thank you, God, for reminding me of what it means to obey immediately."

From then on, my writing took on new meaning. When I was compelled to write about something whether I wanted to talk about that issue or not, I wrote. On days I was running late to work, meeting or activity, I would write immediately and send out the e-missives before leaving the house. I cannot explain it, but those messages sent in the moment like that, time slowed down. Within in whatever brief period I thought I had, a message was typed, edited and sent and I was not late.

"You need to do a blog!" Over and over people said these words.

"Why? Who wants to read that? That sounds like a lot of work, creating the page and then writing in it. Sending these e-missives by e-mail when I am compelled to do it is enough," I would answer.

The pen has been in my hand since I was at least eight years old. I remember that only because of the handwritten booklets I have saved.

Like any other child my imagination was vivid; I just allowed the pen to record it. Every day I wrote in my diary – full conversations with people and doings. In high school these diaries became journals, pages of any day's event. I am still trying to figure out how I had time to write in these journals, be socially active and get some sleep. Oh wait, I am doing that now! God must have been at work then like he is now. Or I had a ton more energy because I was young.

Using a soft flowing black pen on thick lined paper in a notebook was soothing. It was much like how I love to read books that have an inky, papery smell to them, are just the right font size, and smooth pages. If it did not smell or feel right, I did not read it. Mimeograph paper we used to get in school from our teachers was the best to smell. Walking in a lumber store puts my nose in a happy place. It is all about the experience of the physical book and the writing materials more so than what is written.

Transitioning from pen to typewriter, to word processor to computer started out as a challenge. I would still write in cursive and then transcribe the text to type. I would have to do that anyway to send it to a publisher. However, as the technology got better, the computer replaced handwriting. Getting words on paper as fast as my mind thought was fascinating. My love for pen on paper waned, but occasionally when I am not near a computer and need to get something down on paper, I return to my happy space. Vacations are the best place for handwritten pieces that later are typed.

Handwriting, however, still rules at church sermons, travel agent trainings and any other classes or trainings I attend. I wish I still remembered my shorthand. I could get more recorded with that lost skill.

"Let's go to this!" Either Nichole or I said. We were looking at something that told us about a Christian Writer's Conference in California that was given by one of our international churches. It took us no time to register, book a flight and reserve a hotel.

Nichole and I had nothing in common. She was young; I was old enough to be her mom. She was white; I was black. She was single; I was married. God, the Cleveland Church of Christ, and our affinity for writing were our only commonalities. She was writing a book and I was trying to write a book of the collection of e-missives I had done. I took a few pages of that creation in case someone there would take time to read it and give me some creative criticism.

"This will be so cool. I have been wanting to go to a writer's conference. But there are so many out there I haven't been able to determine which one is the right one to go to. So glad this is one our church is giving, then I know it will be what I need to hear," I said to Nichole. She agreed.

It meant flying all the way across the country to a place in a desert in California to the Antelope Valley Christian Writer's Conference.

"Where the heck is this place? We have been driving for a while," Nichole asked.

"According to the map, it should be coming up soon. The names of these streets are crazy! I hope we don't have any problems getting back to the hotel after dark. There are no landmarks to remember or streetlights." My eyes were fixed before me at the plain sandy brown landscape that went on for miles. I started to wonder if this was a good idea or not. We could have gone somewhere closer. I originally liked the idea of coming out there because I had a great deal of family on my mother's side to visit. Any opportunity to travel and visit family or friends is always good for me. Nichole and I visited with my family before we made this drive into the desert. Now, I started to doubt the wisdom of this venture. Two women alone in the desert.

"What a crazy place to put a conference, so far from any hotels. I wonder whose idea that was?" Nichole helped with the navigation, her eyes ever moving to find the way.

"Well it was recommended by our pastor, so it has to be ok."

"True, I am looking forward to seeing why God sent us way out here. We could have gone somewhere in Ohio. Wait!" Her hand flew up. "There is our turn. All these streets look the same and the names are similar too. How does anyone find their way around here?"

I turned the car on that street. Out of the distance a small building appeared. As we got closer, we realized it was a church with a parking lot – all by itself. Seriously? Is *this* the place? I slowly crept the car into the lot, making sure the address matched our confirmation. We were early, the lot was empty.

We were early, but not *that* early. "Where is everyone? It is maybe forty-five minutes or so early. Where are the people who run this thing? Should we get out?" I asked.

"Let's wait to see if anyone else comes." Nichole suggested.

Soon a car or two came; the drivers jumped out and disappeared into the building. We waited for a few more to come before we slipped out of the rental car. It was quiet. *Where did those people go?*

"Can we help you?" someone asked.

"We are here for the writer's conference. Is this the right place?" One of us asked.

"You are at the right place. We are not quite ready, but you are welcome to sit and wait."

"Is Steve here?" We asked in unison. He was the director of the conference and we had had some communication with him before we came. He was a member of one of our sister churches.

"Yeah, let me go get him." the building sucked up the person into its bowels.

"Thank you, Jesus! At least we know Steve *is* here. It seems kind of creepy." I looked around at the artifacts the church displayed. The light brown brick building was bright and welcoming with many rooms. It just seemed so odd to be out in the middle of nowhere.

"Nichole? Juel?" a man asked.

"Yes. Steve?" one of us said.

"So, glad to finally meet you in the flesh. Did you have any problems getting here?" Steve asked.

"Yes, the streets are kind of hard to follow on the map." I said. "We got here so early I thought we might be at the wrong place."

"You *are* at the right place. Registration starts in a few moments. I am so glad you came. It's not often many from church come from out of town." He led us to a place we could sit for a moment. We both sighed as our hearts slowed down. We made it and were ready to discover what needed to happen with our writing.

The conference was for two days in May 2010. Each day was packed with speakers in workshops or general sessions. It began on Friday at 6 p.m. and ended at 8:45 p.m. Saturday started at 8:00 a.m. and ended at 6:00 p.m. Neither of us looked forward to such an early start because we had to drive quite a distance to get there. Thank goodness breakfast and lunch was included for Saturday. God had a reason for us to be in the middle of nowhere. We did not know it yet.

"What did she say?" Nichole and I looked at each with large eyes as we listened to one of the speakers.

"That's not biblically correct." Nichole frowned.

"I know. Are they that accepting out here?" I asked. "We need to find out what's up from Steve." We did not find Steve before we left for the hotel.

"Should we go back tomorrow? Some of the false doctrine stuff I heard has me creeped out." Nichole said, and I agreed.

"I don't know. But at the same time, why would God send us all the way out here if it is not where we need to be? We need to pay attention. We have only tomorrow and then we can get out of here." I said, as we sat on our beds, after getting lost on the way back to the hotel.

We prayed and asked for God's direction whether to go or return to Los Angeles. We stayed.

"Oh, yeah I guess the information doesn't really explain. I am a member of the church, but the people who come to the conference are from all over – various denominations, not just our church." Steve explained during breakfast.

"OOOOH, we thought this was a conference our international church was running and sponsoring. That explains it," I said. It was not what we had planned for, God had us there for a reason. "We almost didn't come back."

Steve laughed. "I am glad you came back; you won't regret it."

And we didn't. Both of us gained much from the speakers.

Sharon, a speaker and author spoke with me and had a chance to read some of the pages I had brought for review. "This is nice, but you need a blog."

A blog? I slumped. "You need to write a blog." I had heard several times from countless of well-meaning friends.

A blog? Why would I do that? Who would read that? I don't have time for that! No matter what excuse I gave, someone would say the "blog" word. Now this author was saying the same thing. *I came all the way to California to hear this again?!*

"Yes, it hones your skills and develops a market of people who read your creations. When you are ready to write a book, then you already have a group of people ready to buy." She said a lot more about how to improve my skills and what a blog looks like, subscribers and more. She showed me her blog and how it benefits her. She had a daily blog. A daily blog, I knew was not for me, but maybe a weekly one crossed my mind.

Oh, my goodness, I am actually thinking about doing this. I thought.

"Yes, I sent others to tell you this, so I had to send you to the desert to hear me clearer," I heard God say. This is so typical of me to not hear God's voice in the middle of what I am doing but hear and see Him so much clearer when I travel. "OK, you know my schedule, since you want me to do this, I will start as soon as I get back. Since it is from you, then it will be great!" I surrendered but wondered how it would work. To write something every week, what a commitment and about what?

On May 17, 2010, my first article in my blog was published, "Advice? Who Needs It–I Do!" The blog was named "Heart Emissions." My dad, girlfriend, Debra, and my son's best friend were my first subscribers. Many more subscribers and followers have been added over the years.

Since that first blog of spiritual devotionals, two other blogs were born. Juel's Travel Beacon, a business blog about travel, peeked its head into the world on February 7, 2015. Various articles written to help travelers enjoy God's world exist. God sent a guest writer who wrote a four-part article that guided travelers on how to pack.

The third blog, "Walking for God Challenge," began on January 1, 2017 and lasted for one year. This blog journalized the 1,500 miles I walked in 2017 to raise $1,550 for HOPE *worldwide*. This blog included a home page, a reason for the challenge page, a page for people to comment on, a journey of the miles walked page, a donor's page, and a page of pictures along the journey. God amazed me by creating the template for this website in a day. I had thought someone professional was going to help me do it, but God did it at my desk. Thanks only to God, he gave me website creation skills while I was a Girl Scout Leader.

As a former reluctant blogger, I now promote others to write blogs.

"I want you all to write either four chapters of a book, four short stories or combination of both," the creative writing instructor told our class. I was probably the oldest one in the class of young adults at Kent State University. I was in my early 50's and pursuing an English Degree.

I loved writing fiction since I was young, and I could make up all kind of scenarios and put them on paper. I played in the world of my imagination alone a lot; it was never lonely.

Four short stories or four chapters? Umm, what to write? *OK, I will write a short story first and then figure out what I want to do later,* I thought. I do not recall the plot of the short story and where it is now stored in my attic, but I do know I got an "A."

During that semester, my husband and I went on an extended weekend vacation to Massanutten Resort in Virginia. On the way during a tropical storm in the dark, only a few miles from our exit, we noticed a car that was driving slowly. The car meandered left then right in the right-hand lane in front of us. When it crept to the left, its wheels rode the dotted white lines of the lane.

"Oh my gosh!" I screamed, as a truck nearly side-swiped the car. The driver had to be either asleep or drunk. We flashed our lights into the back window of the car in hopes that the driver would wake up and pull over. We drove for miles like that flashing in the dark, in the rain; we could barely see. The car would drift left, but not into the next lane, just enough to be close to passing cars. We waited for the impending accident. When the car drifted right, the tires hit the shoulder and then would jump back. Right, left, right, left, flash, flash, flash! We tried to get alongside the car, and we could see the driver with head bowed. Thanks only to God, one of our flashes must have startled the driver. Red brake lights blinked, and a right flashing light appeared on the car to get off at the next exit. As we passed the exiting car, we could only see a shadow, no face, no idea whether it was a male, female or a ghost.

"Thank God, they are getting off!" Dan said. We drove on.

"I wonder what their story is?" I asked. "I am so glad that is over. My heart could not take any more of that. I just knew they would get killed or kill someone else."

That incident spurred the three chapters of my school assignment into life. I wrote the story of that sleeper. That book is still in process, thirteen years later. Only twelve chapters have been written. The first three chapters were read, graded and edited by my teacher and several of the latter chapters have been read by Nichole.

This fiction has been the hardest thing to write. With a full schedule of activities, time to put fingers on a keyboard has been difficult. However, it has been more than just time to write. When something needs to be put on paper via pen or keyboard, it happens. It has not consistently happened with this book. Writing a devotional blog every week has made me realize that writing nonfiction is easier. It was hard, even with notes, to remember what my plot was and the characters.

"Once a book/story is started, no matter how long it takes it will be finished. There is no such thing as starting a story and not ending it." I cannot remember if a teacher told me this or my favorite author, Stephen King in his book on writing said this. I just know it has stuck. So, when I think I need to toss this fiction, I hear that.

The fiction is about adultery and how God works through that. I know in writing this "story" it has been therapeutic, raising up my own personal memories, good and bad. *It must be why I can't get it done, I am still working out my own past involvements,* I kept telling myself. It's a story that must be written, even if it is false; the real story can't be written. It is not even included in this memoir.

"When can we get this done, God? I have people praying for me to get this done." I prayed constantly. I stopped asking people to pray for this book, unless they asked about it.

"I need you to put the fiction down, for a moment, and write *your* real story," I heard during one of my quiet times with God.

"What? It's not time yet. My husband is not ready. I am not ready."

"Yes, now is the time to write the *real* story. The fiction will come later."

Oh, my goodness, for real? Within moments an outline appeared in my notebook – the lives of a gem, the lives that only God and my husband know. *Now?* I thought if ever a book was written about me, it would be after I was famous as a writer. The older I got it did not look like that would happen any time soon. So, it would come after I was dead, and someone read my journals. *Now? While I was a nobody? Who wants to read about a nobody?*

The journey of the lives of a gem began in early 2018. Now you, the reader, I pray are somehow impacted positively spiritually, emotionally and physically. God's timing is always right, even when we do not think so.

When the fiction will be done and what else will be written by Him through me, only God knows. But I am ready to do His will with His talent He has granted me to have.

CHAPTER TEN

THE DEBTOR

*"No one can serve two masters. Either you
will hate the one and love the other, or you will
be devoted to the one and despise the other.
You cannot serve both God and money."
Matthew 6:24.*

I am a female and I *hate* to shop! So why am
I in such debt? I am not trying to say that shoppers
are in debt. My debt is not from shopping; it is
from something else.

My parents gave me an allowance from childhood well into high school. I recorded each entry
in a booklet that I hand-made by stapling three-
ring binder paper, drawing columns with the
amounts I received, the dates, and a running balance. Withdrawals I made for purchases were
recorded and the balance was reduced proportion-
ately with each transaction. There were entries for
loans I made back to my parents when they realized I had accumulated a sum and they needed it.
It was always repaid with interest. It seems I had

little or no intention of spending the money; there was nothing I wanted or needed to save up for. I did buy the occasional candy and treats from the store, but that barely put a dent in the funds I saved. Lunches were my main purchases during my time in high school. Other than that, I had no reason to buy anything. A fashion diva I was not. Any clothes I needed for school were bought by my parents at the start of every school year. My allowance was for my personal spending during the week. I cannot remember if I had specific chores to earn the allowance. Knowing my parents, I probably did. I cannot imagine them giving me money for the fun of it without earning it. That money was hoarded and hidden in some sort of container in my bedroom. It was my intention to never be without money.

"This is the plan," Dan said. "We are going to make sure if we make any charges on our credit cards, that that amount is paid up within thirty days, so we don't have to pay any interest. So, no purchases unless we know we can pay it back within the month." I agreed. I had heard that advice before. It made sense to me then and that is what we did for quite a while.

The first year of our marriage we stayed with my parents to save for a house. Watching our savings account accumulate was our goal to get our own place and move out. It was so easy to save; since we were only paying a small rent to my parents, purchased some food and shared in their food with our young son. It seems we were rolling in dough as we both worked: I had a government agency position and Dan had a union job. Our pay was minimal, but it seemed like tons for us, especially for me after living on allowances. We barely had a reason to use a credit card. We shunned the credit card offers made; we did not see a reason for them. We had maybe one card, just in case, but rarely used it.

Sometime after we moved into our own home (which included a mortgage, utility bills, real estate taxes, home and car insurance, food, clothing, gas for the car and whatever expenses we had to pay to live on), credit cards became a useful tool to fill a short-term gap. Eventually, the plan to pay within a month stretched to two months, three months then whenever.

In the beginning our checking, savings and credit card accounts were joint. Dan managed those accounts. Then something happened: I got my first credit card and my own checking account. I cannot remember why. I know when I had my own travel agency company, Juel's Travel and Cruises, I had a business checking, savings and credit card account to keep our money separate. There was even an escrow account to house the clients' funds that came in so that I could not touch those funds because they belonged to the vendors who supplied me. I opened a separate credit union account somewhere during that time. Part of my government wages were deposited into our joint account and part into the credit union checking for my own spending money. Dan managed the joint account bills and I managed my individual charge card bill and business. Other entrepreneurial ventures came my way, such as Pre-Paid Legal and Premier Designs, Inc. Naturally, separate business accounts were needed for income receipts and expenditures.

Monthly budget ledgers were recorded by both of us for all the accounts and bills that we maintained. We both used those seven to twelve column ledger books. I personally liked the two column red ledger books that featured "budgeted income and expenses" and "actual income and expenses". Dan's recordings are more detailed: twelve columns or more with every bill, with balances due, due dates, payments, and so on. Because electronic technology has overtaken the accounting landscape, it has become increasingly difficult to find the older style print ledgers. We still record information of this sort by hand with a pencil.

I could come up with all kinds of excuses. I could say neither my parents nor anyone else taught me how to be wise in my spending, but that is not true. Both my parents had money, yet they managed it wisely. I was not given everything I wanted. My basic needs were met and that was enough. We lived well, yet, they never overindulged me with stuff. I never experienced worry over not knowing where the next meal was coming from, or whether we would have a roof over our heads or clothes on our bodies. It was always there to use. I was taught to work twice as hard as others because the color of my skin obligated me to produce at a higher level than my counterparts. Proper English, appropriate dress and a positive attitude were the keys.

I could say it is my husband's fault. For most of our marriage, he had union jobs that included periods of unemployment, so I *had* to work. That necessitated having separate accounts and credit cards for the jobs and business ventures where I was involved. But that is not a valid excuse. Yes, I had to work, but that is not a reason for a change in my financial thinking.

I could say being involved in business is at fault. None of those ventures enabled me to retire from my government job, but accumulated expenses that surpassed the incomes. Many of those expenses were charged. But that is not a valid excuse either. I had full control over what should and should not be spent in cash or credit cards. Hoping that somehow it would work out is not a way to run a business.

I could say my addiction to travel is at fault. I jokingly blame my parents for instilling a love of travel in me. I have traveled all my life and must have a fix every quarter. Many of my travels have been on credit cards. But that is no excuse. I should have not traveled if the money weren't in the bank or couldn't be repaid in thirty days. Thanks to God He has helped me with this addiction. He has taught me how to travel enough times during the year without breaking the bank. As a travel agent, I fought the urge to be gone after I help a client travel to their dream vacation.

Over several years, I racked up over fifty thousand in credit card or installment loan debt. This did not include the seventy-five thousand in student loans to send my son and me to college. Making minimum payments meant this debt was going to take an eternity to pay back.

"If I could win a lottery, or if money would fall from heaven for my student loans, I could get six hundred dollars a month back into my pocket. Then I could pay off the credit cards," I told my husband and others many times. Neither of these opportunities happened to me. I continued to pay on these student loans and credit cards. As I type this, these amounts are less, but still substantial.

How is it I can handle other people's monies well, but not my own? I was a business manager for a Girl Scout Day camp. At the end of the camp we had money left over and had to spend it to break even. As a former IRS Agent, I would think I should have been better with my own expenditures while auditing what others did. Crazy! I guess it analogous to the carpenter who builds magnificent homes for his customers but lives in a shack!

"The credit card companies are deceiving you into thinking you have to pay the whole debt off. Contact us and we will help you settle for a lesser amount!"

"Contact us now to remove your debt!"

Commercials blared at me on my radio. I did not want to "remove" my debt; I wanted to pay it off. I did not want them to magically go away as these people implied. That sounded like theft to me. In any case, any debts that are "forgiven" become taxable income on my tax return. I did not have money to pay taxes on any debt forgiven. I would need a loan to do that or pay the IRS in installments which included interest. So, that option was not true forgiveness no matter how enticing it sounded.

Things changed in 2018. Despite my waywardness in spending, God came to my rescue. I guess I learned my lesson well enough. He put me on a "cash only" operation because I had no more credit cards I could use. So, because I was better at spending (because I had no choice), He helped me out. In the winter of 2018, he encouraged me to contact the Christian Credit Counselor, a credit organization that took a few of my credit cards and turned them into one low monthly payment. Interest rates and the required monthly minimums were lowered. I paid the credit counselor; they paid the creditors. All those cards were closed. I was hoping they were going to help with all my credit cards. They were unable to help me with three of the bank credit cards. Bank credit cards were from entities for which there was no possible negotiating. Bummer! I was stuck making the minimum monthly payments on three bank cards – a total debt of $17,800.

In March 2018, God helped me out by sliding me into an eight-car accident on my 62nd birthday. My girlfriend and I were traveling home from a midweek church service on icy roads.

"No, no, we are not really going to be able to stop?" Sonia calmly said, as she braced for impact. A stopped car in the right lane loomed into view. My car tires refused to stop on the icy bridge. We had so much time to see this happen and weren't concerned until we realized my brakes were meaningless. I turned the steering wheel to the left, hoping to miss the car. We missed its rear end but sideswiped it as we continued past. The car bounced off that car and slid into the back of another stopped car in the left lane.

"I hope no one hits us from the back," I said as my eyes stared at the rear-view mirror. Images of tractor-trailer trucks and cars piling up on the highway flashed through my mind. Thanks only to God, no one behind us hit us. They may have hit others or managed to slide between all the stopped cars without hitting anyone.

Neither Sonia nor I were hurt. Sonia did experience minor whiplash, but nothing else. It did not appear anyone else in the accident was injured. Praises to God; it could have been a lot worse. We found out later, a big red pickup truck had started the accident by hitting two cars, then fled the scene.

My front and side were damaged. I had been in accidents before and knew which dealer would do the repairs and that I would have to pay a one-hundred-dollar deductible. So, after the car was towed away, I waited for the dealer to tell me when to pick up the car and pay the deductible. No call came for several days. I called them twice and left messages. Finally, after the third call the car repair representative said, "We are waiting to hear from your insurance company about whether or not they will pay." *What? Why wouldn't they pay?* I thought.

"They are probably going to total your car," My dad told me.

"No way!" I said. *It wasn't that much damage!* I discarded that comment. *He didn't see my car. What did he know?*

"Don't be surprised if they total your car!" Aunt Louise said. *Really?* I thought.

Since she was the second person who said this, I thought, *God are you trying to tell me something? If my car is totaled, how can I afford a new car? I still owe about $3,000 on this car and have no down payment money. This can't be happening.*

Sure enough, they totaled my car and told me to search for a new one. I was unhappy. I was looking forward to having a car with no car note. Now I had to buy another car with a note; a note I had no down payment for. I was driving a Ford Escape. The past three cars were SUV's. I was ready to return to a car; no longer did I have a need for a SUV. Now in my 60's I was only hauling around myself, my grandson and an occasional rider. I found a white 2017 Ford Fiesta. I knew, I had to get a used car because of my financial situation but God granted me with a new car instead.

The insurance company paid the value of my Escape. This value did not cover the full cost of the car; I still owed the $3,000 with my credit union. I did not have GAP insurance. After a conversation with my credit union they were able to grant me a loan for the new car, consolidate another debt I had with them and pull in one of my bank credit cards. The car loan was given to me at an amazing 3% interest rate.

"Thank you, Jesus! God had to put me in a wreck to help me out with my debt!" I told everyone I talked to about the wreck. I still had two bank cards to pay minimum on. I knew somehow those would be worked out in time. I was content with what God had given me in a short two months period – a new car and the major part of my credit debts to be paid off within five years. If I had to pay on the two bank credit cards for however long it would take, so be it.

Everyday junk mail came to our house. Many of them aim to help reduce your credit card debt or consolidate debt. They looked like scams to me. I wanted to consolidate my debt but with a bank. So far, no bank offered me anything; I was a bad risk. Straight to the shredder all these offerings went. The ones with small dollar amounts were the first to hit the shredder. The ones with larger amounts I would linger over and wish: if you could really give me that amount all my cards would be paid off, then I could pay one monthly amount. But I would say, no, and shred it. After a while I got used to seeing the same companies.

One company sent me something every month. I kept wondering why so often. It made me think of the funny story of someone who was caught in a flood and prayed to God for rescue. (I paraphrase here because I can't remember the details.) The man was told originally to leave before the flood, but he said, "No, God's got me." Then when the waters began to rise, someone wading by told him to come with him to safety. He responded, "No, God's got me." Then when he was standing on his roof with the waters all around, someone in a boat came by to rescue him and he replied, "No, God's got me." He drowned. When he went to heaven, he asked, "God, why did you let me drown?" God said, "I sent three people to save you, but you refused their help, so you drowned." This letter in my hand made me do a Better Business Bureau research on the company. In my research, I learned their loans came from a bank, not investors. With trembling fingers, I applied, hoping I was not setting myself up for a scam. I was eligible for $5,000 more than I asked. I said, no, just the amount that I asked for, that was more than enough. Until the amount was deposited into my account, I waited for the scam to happen; it didn't. I paid off those two bank credit cards. Hallelujah!

The extra blessing, the excess was put in savings. Traveling with a team from our church to Indonesia for a mission trip was in my dreams. I scrapped pennies toward that goal. Now, I had the money to cover the $1,000 cost for air, the most expensive ticket I had ever purchased. I asked for help with my debt, but God gave me more.

With only two credit cards open—both with zero balances--I should have been ready to live the repentant life on a cash basis. That was my intention, but that is not what happened.

By September of 2019, those two zero balance cards had accumulated debt, probably from indulging my travel obsession, and who knows what all else I thought I needed to buy on credit. I realized in late August, while preparing to pay my September bills, I was not going to have any money for personal spending. Every dime of my pension was going towards a bill. The Holy Spirit told me "take those two cards and give them to the Credit Christian Counselor." I made the necessary contacts. The card accounts were eventually closed, and they were rolled into my existing re-payment program. This adjustment meant, however, that my monthly payments would increase by one hundred eighty-four dollars, first installment of which was due the next day. *Oh, my goodness! How the heck can I get that amount in one day?*

I prayed more than I ever that somehow, I would get the one hundred eighty-four dollars before the fifteenth since I had to "steal from Peter to pay Paul". In other words, I had to borrow from another bill that automatically came out of my account on the fifteenth. On that same day, I went through all my automatic bill withdrawals and other monthly expenditures to see which ones I needed to stop having, luxuries that I needed to get rid of. Twenty-seven dollars monthly for gym membership was first. It was a small amount, but it would help towards that one hundred eighty-four dollars.

Forty dollars a month was paid towards Prepaid Legal for a legal plan I used when I needed legal services. I did not want to let this go since I do use this plan occasionally for business and personal purposes. However, I had to do something now and this needed to go! I called the company and explained I needed to cancel. I was told I needed to send an e-mail to confirm my cancellation. The operator asked, "aren't you an associate of the company?"

"Yes, but I haven't sold anything in years." I responded.

"There is some money in your account." She said.

"Money? For what?"

"I don't know, but I can only see it. You must call the associate department to find out and get it. I can only deal with your plan."

What? How can I have money? Yeah, back in the day I used to get a residual income from people I sold the plan to, but I haven't got a check in the mail in years. What is she talking about?

I called the associate side of the company.

"We have been looking for you. The bank account number we have is no longer good and has been rejecting any incomes we have for you," the man said. He mentioned a name of a bank I never heard of before. I guessed that must have been a bank that bought out another bank years ago, or I never knew the real name of the bank that owned my home bank. "We have $465.45 on hold for you."

Four hundred sixty-five dollars and forty-five cents? Oh my gosh! God you answered my prayer on the same day that I pleaded for help! It was not a lot of money, but at that moment it seemed like millions of dollars. I only needed one hundred eighty-four dollars and he gave me more! The amount enabled me to have spending money for September, tithes and put ten percent in savings. I told this story to everyone I met.

October came. I did not think about the one hundred eighty-four dollars increase applied for all the months left in the program. I did not have the money. But somehow in October, November, December, January and the first two weeks of February 2020, God gave me enough money to pay it and for spending. I can't explain it. I just know it happened.

While God was providing for my needs, He taught me financial lessons. Many of the lunch/dinner dates on my schedule were either cancelled because I did not have the money, someone paid for my meal, or I had the person(s) come to my house for a meal instead. The meals I made in my home were the best! I had so much more fun with whoever I was supposed to be going out with in our home. Being a hostess was a delight. It cost me nothing since the food was already in the house and I loved to cook. The conversations were more enlightening because there were no inhibitions about talking loudly, laughing, or speaking about something we did not want the rest of the restaurant to know. I decided I need to have people more often in our house instead of going to a restaurant.

I knew I needed a part-time job. Waiting for God to get me through every month was not acceptable. I needed to play a part in my repentance. Preparing a resume was the hardest part. It has been years since I had a resume. Applying for jobs online was also tedious. What should I apply for? How many hours could I work? Who should be my references? Looking for a job took time out of my busy schedule; but it had to be done. I told my closest friends in church and all the ladies in BSF to pray for me to find part time employment. I found telling people about this financial sin to be a freeing experience and it helped others realize what changes they needed to make in their own financial lives. It also helped others see I did not have it as *"together"* as they thought.

As I mentioned before, I had complained to others about the six hundred dollars a month in cash I would have back in my account when my student loans were paid. I made it seem like that was the reason I was so broke. But during these five months the severity of my sin opened my eyes. The Holy Spirit prompted me to see when all the debts would be paid, that were not student loans. Those three pockets of debt reduction that God set up for me in 2018 meant that, in three separate months in 2023, money would return to my pocket. I would get a raise! Nine hundred sixty-seven dollars would be credited early in the year, five hundred eighty-two dollars and thirty-three cents more would be applied in the middle of the year, and a final five hundred ninety-six dollars and seventy-two cents would be applied in the latter part of 2023. By the end of the year, a total of $2,146.05 a month, would stay in my bank account!

Oh, my Lord, what a sinful wretch I have been! I had thrown away so much money that could have been used for Your purposes, to help others, to save, to do whatever instead of being used to pay off personal debt and interest! That six hundred dollars I have boo-whooing about is pittance in comparison to this! With this back in my account, the student loan will go down faster, and savings will increase! This time I am repentant for real! No going back! Forgive me, I am sorry! How could you give me so much and I have been so wasteful?

Now I am on a "cash only" living style. If I do not have the cash, I cannot buy it. It is so freeing to say, "Sorry, can't do it…can't buy it…don't have the money." If it is something I really need, somehow God enables it to be purchased. He even gave me part time employment at Chick-fil-A® where I can serve customers as a hostess. That is fun, energetic, and never dull.

I received my first paycheck Friday February 14, 2020. My prayer was to have a net of five hundred dollars a month after taxes to get through each month. That first check, and the second one two weeks later, showed me my God, my special

Valentine, surpassed that request. In February, more money came: federal and state tax refunds and the largest commission check I have ever received in all my years as a travel agent.

For the first time in all my days, there was no stress on how to spend the funds. Each check was distributed as follows: fifty percent was applied evenly (ten percent each) among five categories: tithes, special missions, savings, investments, and then on me. What remained was applied to bills. Such a simple way to spend God's money was granted to me. Thank you, God, for allowing me another chance to be an excellent steward of the funds You give me.

Then COVID-19 came. On March 15, 2020, Governor Mike DeWine shut down all dine-in restaurants. After only six weeks at Chick-fil-A®, I filed for unemployment for the first time since I was in my twenties. I was a dining room hostess and was unwilling to work in the kitchen or at the drive through window. Thanks to God's financial plan monies are sitting in checking and savings for such a time as this. God provided an unexpected bonus. Six months of student loans under the CARES Act were deferred by the government. However, I continued to make the monthly payments because there was zero interest on the payments. This results in $2,049.48 reduction in the principal in 2020. The $1,200 stimulus check and the Pandemic Unemployment Assistance payments were allocated to the five categories and the rest to bills. God's financial plan even in a pandemic works.

CHAPTER ELEVEN

THE FRIEND

"A man of many companions may come to ruin, but there is a friend who sticks closer than a brother." Proverbs 18:24

I was born a wallflower. Standing along a wall, observing, and listening to others is what I prefer to do. It is difficult for me to engage in one-on-one conversations. It is easier for me to stand on a stage in front of a million people and give a speech than to interact with one person. I was not shy, just quiet. I was not afraid of people; I just didn't want to look bad, odd, weird, whatever. However, being quiet made me weird anyway.

"You are such a quiet person; you are going to have to come out of that if you want to move up in the organization," one of my favorite bosses told me. Because of him I was encouraged to enroll in Toastmasters at our workplace. Every week I had to stand before a group and do some sort of speech from impromptu speeches to researched and prepared speeches. Nervousness flipped my stomach; even when I began to love doing this, there was always nervousness. I love public speaking. With years of various types of public presentations under my belt, I still have those little flip flops in my stomach. I welcome that slight uneasiness, because to be cocky about going before the public can be disastrous. I prefer the uncertainty of acceptance until I am a few words in and God gives me the confidence I need to finish.

Being a friend is hard. It requires one-on-one communication, which is unscripted, unplanned, random and vulnerable. I do not remember how Cheryl, Susan and I met; they are my longtime forever friends. Cheryl and I played in the streets together when we were in early elementary. We lived cattycorner across the street from each other. So, we might have known each other before we started kindergarten. We did everything together; I liked doing the same things. She was light-skinned with long copper braids. I loved the color of her hair and wished mine were the same. We played with dolls, spent hours at each other's homes and slept overnight a lot. My parents moved me from her to a residence to the other side of town. We kept in touch for as long as we could, but like all long-distance relationships it was hard; now we keep in contact occasionally or on Facebook. We are still friends, just not as close.

I met Susan in that move to the other side of town. We were polar opposites. She was tall, light skinned, dainty with long black plaited hair down to her waist. I was shorter, brown skinned, with short shoulder length hair and a tom boy. I loved to wear dresses even as I climbed the nearest tree. The view from the top of a tree is beautiful and peaceful. This was the perfect quiet place to watch people without them knowing I was watching them.

"You are too old to be roller skating in the streets!" Susan told me once when I was around twelve years old. I looked down at my steel skates that clamped on my shoes at the toes, which held my foot in with a metal plate at my heel and was buckled across the top of my foot with a strap. *Too old?*

"No, I am not! This is fun!" I stuck my lip out. I kept on skating. Our differences drew us closer. We had one thing in common; we loved to read. Reading is the only thing that made me sit still for long periods of time. Otherwise I was up and moving.

Susan lived around the corner from me. We had to walk past houses, a store and a bar to get to each other's homes. Walking, skating or riding a bike were my mode of transportation, even when she told me I was too old to skate or bike. I did it anyway. I rode that bike everywhere.

The seventh grade separated us. The junior high school district line pulled us apart for three years. She went to Nathan Hale Junior High and I went to Robert H. Jamison Junior High.

"Mom! What is this?" I handed her a notice about my Junior High School placement. "It says I HAVE to go to Nathan Hale! I don't WANT to go THERE!! Nathan Hale? That old grungy school? I don't want to go there! Those kids are rough there! I can't survive there. I will get beat up every day!"

"No, worries; we will go to the school and get this straightened out!"

My mom and I walked into that school. It was like walking into a building that was made of one huge, wide endless hall with rooms off it. The ceiling in that hallway looked like the height of the building; it looked dark and scary. It did not want me there and I did not want to be there.

"So sorry, Mrs. Taylor, your house is right on the border line and we made a mistake. Juel will be going to Robert H. Jamison. We will make the correction."

"Whoosh! Thanks, mom!" I said as we left. I was not going there. It never dawned on me to be concerned for my best friend who was going there. She told me as an adult she survived because she had four brothers who protected her. We were reunited when we went to John Adams High School. During those three years we added new friends to our duo.

Sometime in junior high, three new friends were added to my circle of friends – Darlene, Robin and Vanessa. The four of us were always together. Occasionally Susan joined us. With these three we practiced the new craze – line dancing – all the time. After a while it got difficult to keep up with the plethora of line dances that came out, but we tried hard to keep up.

"Ain't he cute?!" One of us exclaimed about one of the members of the Jackson 5. We were official members of the "J 5 Fan Club." We danced to every album and swooned over them. We were too broke to attend concerts, but we watched every show or concert they performed on TV.

In addition to dancing, we liked to sing.

"Let's do it!" Our foursome and another friend Pam said. "We can sing a gospel song in the school talent show."

"Peace Be Still" was the song of choice. We practiced and practiced. We sounded pretty good. For a reason I do not remember I missed one of the practices close to the time of the show. I was booted out. Our group was serious about making practices. I do not remember if I missed only one or more, but I know I was not on stage; I watched from the audience. Maybe I did not really want to do it, because I do not remember feeling hurt or left out. It was just something else on my schedule to do. The group did a fantastic job at the talent show; they did not win, but it was fun anyway.

Vanessa, Robin, Darlene and I were tight in high school and remain friends into our sixties. We loved to dance at parties and get the attention of boys. We were quite different in personalities; just like with Susan I think that is what kept us together – opposites attract, like kinds repel. I am in more contact with Susan than the other three as an adult. Susan and I spend time at breakfast and lunches to reconnect with our grandchildren. Vanessa, Robin, Darlene and I stay connected by phone and occasional visits. Darlene moved to California right after we graduated from high school. Many times, I flew miles to visit her in California. She always had a coupon for any meals we ate at restaurants. I will miss seeing her when God enables me to visit California; I will have to buy meals at retail. She is the first one of us to die – April 7, 2017. It is still hard to believe she is not here.

Being a friend as an adult is different. It was easier as a minor because we were thrown together in classes and somehow friends develop on their own. As an adult it is not quite that way. I was not an initiator then; even now I always fight my own insecurities about talking with strangers. Maybe I can blame my parents and other adults – "don't talk to strangers." No, that is not it; it is not natural for me to initiate. That wallflower that wants to watch, listen and observe reigns inside.

"Just put out your hand and say, 'Hi my name is Juel, what's yours?'" I was taught in my early forties after I became a baptized disciple how to be an initiator. It is always difficult, but a lot easier than when I was younger.

The years before baptism, it was like being in school. My relationships were coworkers and Boy and Girl Scout leaders. In both scenarios I was put with people because of a job or Scout activity and friendships happened. Many of those friends I remain in contact with through Facebook while others I have no idea if they are alive or dead; those were for a season. Traveling to visit one or more of these long-time friends is pure joy as we recount the craziness we did in Scouting or in the workplace. Some of that craziness I thank God, He forgave me of. However, the majority of what we did was pure fun, laughter, and enrichment. When God made me realize how much Scouting had become my god, I was removed from that endeavor, but He allowed me to remain friends with many of them, friends I can laugh and cry with as we age.

Friendships after Scouting were through church, job or business. I did not have time for joining clubs or other outside activities. I was a church worker, parent, wife, a business owner and a coworker. My deepest friendships were and still are from church. With my girlfriends I can confess my deepest sin, pray and watch God free me of my selfishness and live life His way. I do not know where I would be if I didn't have these women in my life to encourage, correct and comfort me. My marriage would be nonexistent, and I would be miserable.

During a period of weight gain, I was given friends through attending Weight Watchers sessions and being a Weight Watchers Leader. Losing weight together and sharing each other's stories bond me with many friends. God made me a more confident person after losing the weight. Keeping the weight off is a daily challenge for the rest of my life, such as walking with God is a daily challenge. With friends the walk is easier to endure.

Walking miles with friends on pavement has been the most delightful. While losing weight I discovered I love walking miles for fun, to lose and to maintain. Training for a long-distance race or walking in a race with friends is refreshing and revealing. The endorphins that are stirred up remove walls of inhibition. We talk and talk about so many intimate issues in our lives that sitting at a table in a restaurant would prevent. Time and the miles do not exist; we are always amazed at how far we walked and how much time has passed. It never feels like we were together that long.

I was never the popular girl, but I do have a lot of friends. I pray that the friends I have had the pleasure of knowing, God has enabled me to be a positive impact on. For those that I have hurt, I pray they have forgiven me. For those to come, I pray I can be the best friend they ever had.

CHAPTER TWELVE

THE SCUBA DIVER

"And God said, 'Let the water teem with living creatures . . .' So God created the great creatures of the sea and every living and moving thing with which the water teems, according to their kinds, . . . And God saw that it was good."
Genesis 1:20-21.

Born under the sign of a Pisces, I love to be in and near water. However, I had a fear of deep water. It took me three classes with three teachers to learn how to swim as an adult in my forties.

"I have always wanted to be a scuba diver." My husband grinned as he spoke. "I watched 'Jacque Cousteau' and 'Sea Hunt' as a kid and wanted to be one. However, because I was black the opportunity seemed impossible."

Danny is a fish! His parents put him in Lake Erie with a life preserver as a child and he has been a self-taught swimmer ever since. He and the water are one; he can hold his breath for long periods of time without a struggle.

I can swim, but I am not a fish. I always must remind myself if I get in trouble I can float and swim on my back. I am not as comfortable as I want to be, like Danny; I still need to take lessons to improve on what I do know, learn new strokes and become more relaxed in the water. Snorkel, mask and fins are my source of security in the water.

Jamaica was the first location we had a chance to snorkel. Dan and I took a small boat out with a company into clear water with lots of visibility. With the snorkel, mask and fins they provided we gasped at the multitude of colorful fish and coral. I fell in love with gazing at God's underwater nature. The warm water and buoyant salt were relaxing and refreshing. With the sun on our backs, our eyes met eye-to-eye with yellow, orange, blue and other colorful fish that caressed our flesh. We did not want to get out. Snorkeling close to shore later in the week did not have the same effect, nor the same clarity or calmness. Fighting waves and seeing less fish made us pant for more snorkeling in deeper waters near coral.

During that boat ride, Dan dove down and held his breath while I watched. I tried a few times, but I could not stay down as long especially with the life preserver doing its job of keeping me up. Dan let some of his air out and was able to go deep or was just able to stay down in spite of the preserver. I was not taking any chances of drowning in the ocean where I couldn't touch the bottom. On one of his breath dives, I saw him looking at something at the bottom intently. He got really close, then all of a sudden, his head popped back, and he swam to the surface.

"Did you see that?" he asked while we treaded water.

"See what?"

"That fish."

"What fish, there are a lot of them."

"I saw something laying on the bottom in the sand and dove down to take a look. I thought, 'aw a dead fish.' Then it moved! I realized then it was one of those flat fish that looks like it is laying on its side with both eyes on the same side. That was cool!"

Relaxing and mesmerizing is what snorkeling is. We could not get enough. Once we were back home, we took a snorkeling class, so we could be excellent at snorkeling. In the class we swam in lanes. At the same time, we noticed dark moving shadows in other lanes below us – scuba divers! Our mouths dropped! We were so busy watching them that sometimes we missed instructions from the teacher. It looked like the divers were having a lot of fun learning how to scuba dive. We wanted to take that class, especially Dan, it would be his dream come true!

Somehow, we found a course. Another woman from church joined us, Loretta. There were three dive companies in our local area. We took the snorkel course with one dive company but enrolled in the scuba diving course with another company. We were planning to take the course with the company we took the snorkel lessons with. However, a flyer at the swimming pool that Dan, Loretta and I swam at offered lessons for a scuba diving course with a different company. So, since that course was going to be in the same place, we regularly were swimming in, we jumped on it! God sent us the best!

The three of us took a Discover Scuba course, liked it and moved into the full scuba diving course. There were about fifteen of us in the course, predominately African Americans. The course was spearheaded by an African American diving club that was encouraging minorities to scuba dive. We were in class for weeks! We had to obtain book knowledge and water application knowledge in order to pass the course. It was hard!

"Thank goodness the three of us are doing this together," I said. "Danny is the fish and can help Loretta and I with the water skills. Loretta and I then can help each other and Danny with the book knowledge. Where one is weak, the other is strong, and we help each other. Without you two, I know I wouldn't be able to pass this course. I would have quit long time ago!"

"I am glad, Dan is here, too." Loretta said. "The water skills are tough! I wouldn't make it without him!"

We practiced in the water; we practiced for the written quizzes, then the test. There was testing in the water and testing at a desk. We were in school as adults and it was fun. These tests were important; any small thing done wrong could mean death or permanent impairments. It seemed to take forever for us to finish that course. We had heard of other courses that only took a few weeks or a few days to be certified. We quickly learned that our dive master was thorough. He wanted to make sure his certified divers were prepared for any situation and would survive. We thanked God he sent this dive master because if we had taken a shorter course we would not have been as informed. We both loved and hated it.

"Oh my gosh, this is so heavy! Why are we doing this?" one of us moaned as we approached the quarry's edge. Once we were in the water, the equipment we wore did not feel so heavy anymore. We trained in the pool and then eventually in a quarry filled with fish and other items for us to see. There were platforms 40 feet down where we would do certain underwater skills with our breathing, masks, Buoyancy Control Device (BCD), compass and other tools and skills. Most quarries also had sunken items for us to find and see.

Once while swimming a course with a compass, on my way back it seemed I lost my sense of direction. I was not sure if I was looking up or down; it was kind of weird. I panted more than I wanted. Finally, I saw the platform approaching in the murk, but was disoriented. At the platform, as I held onto the rope that held the platform in place, with my other hand I grabbed the regulator in my mouth, I could not breathe.

Oh my gosh! I need air! I need to take this regulator out, so I can get some air! I thought.

The regulator is what brings air from the tank on my back to my mouth. My eyes got as big as saucers; I was told by the dive master. It seems I became two people. While one hand was trying to remove the regulator, the other hand pressed that hand down against the regulator to keep it in place. The dive master motioned me with his hand to slow my breathing down, "slow, calm down!" I slowed my breathing and relaxed. I hung there for a few minutes realizing I had just had a panic attack underwater, not a good place to have an attack! The dive master let me regroup and then we surfaced. I am still amazed at how my mind honestly believed if I removed my source of air, I would live.

After Dan, Loretta and I passed our written, underwater skills and the swim tests we became certified scuba divers. It was the hardest skill I have ever learned, but one of the most rewarding to be able to see God's underwater creation up close and personal.

Our first real dive after certification happened in the Grand Caymans. Loretta, Dan and I went on a cruise with a group of friends and booked a dive at that island. It was all that I had imagined and more. The buoyancy of the warm saltwater was perfect! It was so much easier and relaxing in saltwater instead of the fresh water we trained in. Plus, we could see further because of the clarity and we were warm. We trained in cold water. We dove deeper than we did in training as we followed the dive master and the rest of the members of our tour. It was rough not being able to linger at some of God's creations to stay with the group. The leader, however, did make stops and point out interesting sights.

It was always a bit scary thinking about how we were placing ourselves on the food chain and paying cash to do it. Any small mistake on our part could end our days of breathing on land. Colors of all kinds in fish and coral surrounded us. I thanked God for allowing us to see his underwater world together. It was worth the weeks of agonizing training to get here. The three of us were shocked at the lack of experience/knowledge some of the divers had. Our dive master had warned us of people who had taken abbreviated courses and how they were a risk in the water to self and others. It was obvious! We had gone deep enough where we needed to make a stop halfway up to remove the gases that had built up in our bodies. Many shot past us in a hurry to get above water – maybe they were running out of air; I don't know, but I prayed they wouldn't suffer from the bends or any other ill effect of returning to the surface too fast. Besides, we were not ready to end this adventure in the sea.

The three of us had non-stop chatter back on the cruise ship. Our cruise mates, including Loretta's husband, smiled and were interested, but could not fully understand our excitement. It was the best thing we did on that cruise. I cannot even remember what we did on the other islands. I know we spent it with the others because we did not want to make the whole trip a dive trip and not exclude out friends; even though we wished we could have especially after that dive.

Dan and I had several more dives after that on other cruise ship sailings. One of our most memorable one was while on vacation for our nephew's wedding in California. We had the rare opportunity to dive in cold saltwater in La Jolla. We were warned we had to have cold water training to do the dive and we had to swim from the beach to the dive spot which was over 100 yards out. Now we saw the importance of why we had to pass the 200-yard swim test as part of the scuba diving course. The difference here was we swam against the waves. That was exhausting! Our group had to take our time getting out there, so we would not be too tired to dive.

On this trip we stayed up in the mountains. Because of traffic or something else, we were the last ones to arrive. Everyone's eyes were on us! We were the only blacks in the group. I could hear them thinking: "black people – always late!" I am an on time, painfully early type of person and I did not like this feeling of being on the spot in front of strangers, especially white people!

"Here is your equipment, be quick about getting it together, we are about ready to go!" The dive master said gruffly.

Dan and I within what seemed like seconds, snapped, slapped, twisted all our equipment together. A look of bewilderment came on the dive masters face, as if he had saw something strange. "Where did you say you were from?" he asked.

"Cleveland, Ohio" we said in chorus.

"Oh, so you *have* had cold water diving. You will have no problems with this water at all!" A small grin came on his face.

As our group walked on the beach to the water, the dive master yelled out at many of them. "Don't drag my equipment! You are getting sand in it!" He looked at us and he saw we carried everything off the ground. We had no intentions of getting sand in his equipment or ours. A big grin came on his face. He came over to us. "I am so glad you two are experienced. The rest of these people are going to mess up my gear."

We both sighed with relief. We had earned the respect of the dive master, no matter what the others thought. We began that long swim out watching fish, stray kelp and beached black seals. We also prayed a shark would not mistake us for a seal and take a bite. At the drop zone we dove fifty to sixty feet. The kelp is amazing – tall, ferny, tree like greenery under water! We all had dive knives in case of entanglement. Someone later told us they saw a big shark, but Dan and I missed it because we were near the end of the pack and it had swum off. I wanted to see a shark, but not close enough to do me any harm. I was happy, yet disappointed.

The water was not cold. After a time, Dan and I got hot. We could not talk about it in the water, but later we both said we were burning up. The heavy mill wetsuits we had on were toasty! It was because we were used to water much colder that the Pacific. Lake and quarry water in the north is frigid. We have been in water where our lips turned blue. This water felt like bath water to us. We laugh about that often. No wonder the dive master said we would have no problems in the "cold" water.

Sometime during that dive, I had to tell the dive master I was near the air level he wanted us to return to the surface. Dan had plenty of air. He was so relaxed; his breathing was slow. I had a few buoyancy issues and had gulped down more air than I wanted. So, with a few others I slowly rose to the surface and swam back with the waves to the shore. Dan and the rest of the group soon followed. We were all so beat after the dive. The swimming and the maneuvers underwater burned up any fuel we had eaten for breakfast. Dan and I had a good hour drive back to our resort. We were tired but loved every minute of that time in the Pacific. Every time I am in La Jolla, I look down into that bay and remember the joy of God's nature below those waves.

I had dreams of becoming a dive master and training others to be scuba divers. I loved to teach adults, and this seemed like a perfect fit. However, as the years sped past, several dives later and watching one of our dive masters get the bends repeatedly while trying to help students, I changed my mind. It was too dangerous to be a dive master. Diving with my husband was enough.

That too eventually changed. The cost of scuba diving is not cheap! We purchased wet suits of various thicknesses based on the temperature of

the water, BCD's, dive computers, regulators,
fins, snorkel, mask, four air tanks and other acces-
sories for the both of us. We wanted our own
equipment, especially the regulator and snorkel
because we did not trust the dive companies'
cleanliness. The equipment and the tours cost a
lot! Our cost is whatever times two! We had to
strategically choose what trips we could afford.

I soon learned that even though I loved being
in the water and diving down to see God's world,
it was not one of my top twenty things to do. It
was just another thing I like to do with my husband, but it was not high on the list. Scuba diving
for Danny is high on his list since it was a childhood dream. I had to realize that what I thought
was my dream, was really his dream and had to
back off diving because of other things I wanted
to do. I encouraged him to dive with friends without me while I snorkeled or did something else.
But he never went without me. After our Scouting
obsession, I did not want this to become another
obsession for me with a huge price tag on it that
we should not be paying.

I was heavier when I learned to dive and
needed more weights to pull me down. I often
wonder, now that I am smaller, how much in
weights I would need. It will have to remain a
wonder. God is not calling me to take on that activity again. I continue to use my snorkel, mask
and fins for swimming in pools and in the ocean.
I had to sell some of my equipment because of the
lost weight and get smaller light-weight wetsuits
for warm water snorkeling. Putting a tank on my

back and regulator in my mouth has not led me in that direction. I love watching scuba divers on TV doing rescue dives or whatever they do and checking out their equipment and remembering, that used to be us.

Loretta, however, left us in the dust! She became an advanced scuba diver almost to the point where she could take courses to be a dive master. She dives every year in a warm climate location and dives regularly in our cold-water areas in the US and Canada. Every time I see her pictures or talk with her, I get an urge to return, but not enough to do it! It is not my dream, just another thing I have done that I enjoy.

I often feel I have kept Dan from his dream since I will not go with him. But if that is something he really wants to do; he would do it. So, I cannot allow myself to regret my pulling out. It's Dan's dream; he must live it! Maybe, what he has lived is enough and he does not need to go any further because he had that chance that he never thought he would as an African American.

God gave Dan and me a gift of those few short years in that mysterious world of great sea creatures, foliage and coral to experience together. He gave us a gift of working and learning together. He gave us a gift of binding us closer in our union. He gave us more than we could have imagined for such a time as then.

CHAPTER THIRTEEN

THE HAIR CHANGER

"Your beauty should not come from outward adornment, such as braided hair and the wearing of gold jewelry and fine clothes. Instead, it should be that of your inner self, the unfading beauty of a gentle and quiet spirit, which is of great worth in God's sight." I Peter 3:3-4.

From as far back as I can remember, it has always been about The Hair.

"What the heck did you do?" my mother screamed.

The smile that covered my face as I combed my straight black and brown hair, dropped into a straight line of confusion. "Uh? What are you talking about?"

"Your hair! What did you do to it?!"

Do to it? I thought. *It looks great to me! Why is she so upset?* "Well, I thought since I am old enough, I took the ironing comb and straightened it." I was too afraid to say it looked great or ask her how she felt. It was obvious. *What did I do wrong?* She took me to the beautician every other week to be straightened. So, it could not have been she did not like it straight.

"You burned your hair out! It is shorter than it should be! You had the comb too hot!"

What? Yeah, I had felt the usual burn on my scalp when the hot comb slid through my hair, but that was normal. *Burned out? What is she talking about?*

"Look! Look in the mirror!" She turned me bodily towards the mirror.

"Huh?" it looked ok to me, nice, straight and shiny.

"Look at this picture of what your hair normally looks like." She pushed a picture in my face. The hair was straight shiny and hung just below my shoulders. I looked back at myself in the mirror; now it hung at about ear length. *How did I miss that? Wow!* I loved the feel of my hair on my neck and now there was none.

"I am sorry! I should have asked you first. I just thought I could do it myself." Tears rolled down my face. "I won't do it again!"

"No need to punish you, having shorter hair is punishment enough! Don't you ever touch that iron again. You could have burned the house down!!" She rushed out looking bigger than normal.

I did not touch my hair again until I was an adult, too afraid I would mess up again.

My hair journey began with braids. My mother braided it, although I do not remember her doing it. I have heard others telling of how much it hurt getting it combed, brushed and braided. I do not remember a thing. Either I have blocked that out in my memory because it was so painful or maybe it was not painful at all. I wish I could ask my mother about that, whether I was tendered-headed or not.

"I don't remember you screaming and hollering about getting it done. That was a different time and place, children knew their place and didn't complain." My dad told me when I asked about this daily experience. "She braided and corn rolled your hair."

So, if there was any pain, I accepted it. I have a high pain tolerance.

But I do remember when I had to comb my own daughter's hair. I hated it! Patience for combing her thick long black hair did not exist for me. I wanted to get it done as fast as possible and move on to something else. She screamed and yelled all the time as I raked the comb through her hair. She loved it when her dad did it. He was patient, gentle and talkative with her. Not a tear fell from her eyes. She was glad when I did not have time to take care of her hair. Because of my experience, I did not take her to the hairdresser to have perms or other straightening ingredients put in her hair. I wanted her hair to be as natural and long as can be without chemicals. This also meant I had to comb that hair instead of making it easier if I paid someone else to do it. There would have been fewer tangles to deal with and less crying. I felt it was worth it so that she would not go through what happened to me.

Eventually, my mom took me to a hairdresser. My hair was thick, but after the hair burn out by me, it became thin. How I longed for my hair to be below my shoulders again. That never happened until a much later time in life. Chemicals were put in my hair to make it straight and keep it that way for at least a month. With thick hair that tended to curl on its own, mom needed it straight. I am sure it was a workout for her. At first, she had the hairdresser straighten it with a hot iron comb and hot curlers – press and curl. The heat pressing on my scalp and leaving a mark with iron or curler was a standard feel. "Sorry baby, I got too close." my hairdresser often said. Feeling the breeze blow through my curls was delightful afterwards. However, if I walked in a fog or in the rain, it shrunk into a ball of tangled, wool; sometimes I looked like a boy. If this happened the same day or soon after my hair was done, both my mother and I were mad – what a waste of money. Plus, I hated how I looked, not like a girl at all; I felt ugly.

I guess my mom had enough of that and had the hairdresser apply chemicals to my head.

"Hold still, no matter how much it burns you gotta hold still! It needs to set. Don't you dare scratch your scalp while it is happening or scratch it before you come to the next appointment. It will not be good for you if you do!" Scratch is all I wanted to do but did not. The burn was bad enough; I did not want it any worse.

It was always worth it! My unmanageably curly hair was curly or straight and shiny for weeks. In the rain I wore a protective rain scarf just in case. This was more expensive than a hot comb du; I did not want my mom to get mad at me and I did not want my hair to be jacked up in front of my friends.

"What the heck is happening!" I screamed looking at the hair in my hand. "Mom! Look at this!"

Mom's mouth dropped. One side of the hair on my head was shorter than the other. Conclusion, the hairdresser had put too many chemicals in my hair, and it was falling out! Mom fired her and got someone else. My hair had to be cut to make it even. Relying on and finding good hairdressers was a chore. Once you found a good one, you never let them go. You drove miles to get to them. As an adult I drove to a hairdresser forty-five minutes away in Akron; no one else in Cleveland met my needs.

As an adult, I continued with hairdressers. I stopped having chemicals put in my hair. Between the pain at application and the fear of it falling out again, I returned to having it pressed. Soon the flat iron came out. Instead of a hot comb, two long flat hot metal pieces connected by a two-prong handle that opened and closed the metal to slide hair between and straighten. This was faster than using the hot comb which required using smaller sections of hair to comb; a flat iron could flatten a whole length of hair from scalp to end. Time sitting in the chair was lessened.

Sitting in the chair, however, was not the real issue about going to a hairdresser. The appointment took forever, no matter what time the appointment was for or what was being done. I hated waiting with other ladies to get my hair done. At some places I waited hours before my hair was washed, let alone blow-dried and pressed. I could never understand this. It was a social time for many of the ladies. It was a time for me to read a good book, though I'd rather be at home reading not in a salon.

Soon I divorced salon hairdressers and ventured into stylists who did hair in their home. This was better. I was the only one scheduled at a time, no wait time, just conversation while she washed, blow-dried and pressed it – quick, simple and often cheaper.

With a press and curl I still could not walk in a fog or rain – an instant Afro would be the results if I did not protect it with a rain scarf or waterproof hat. This worked in my favor when wearing Afros and Afro puffs were in. I stopped going to hair stylist altogether when I wore an Afro. I wore it proudly with black power. My Afro was huge! Having the largest Afro possible was always ideal for everyone then. When my hair was at its maximum height, it felt light and I could feel the wind blow on my scalp as it blew in the wind. Long tooth afro picks of various colors and styles with a huge black fist on the end racked my hair every day to keep it in shape. The style looked so easy, but it was not. I had to braid it every night for it to be as tall as possible during the day. That was time consuming. All day long I patted it into shape and picked it out with the afro pick. Leaning against something or laying down meant a flattened look on the side the hair was mashed in. Sleeping in a fro was not optional unless I wanted it flat and unmanageable in the morning. Guys loved it when we girls braided their hair to get that bigger than life look as their crowns. I braided Dan's hair all the time. He braided it most of the time but loved it better when I did it. Braiding the back is harder to do by yourself.

With the afro I still had to protect it from fog and rain. Starting the day with a tall afro might mean coming home with a shrunken boy cut afro at the end of the day if it got wet! It's amazing how low and tight the hair can get in a few seconds.

"I would go to school with my hair in a huge afro. At my school we had a dress code, no hair below the ear line." Dan tells this story often. "When I get to school, the principal would send me home to cut my hair. I would go home apply some water to it and come back to school with a short neat afro and he would be satisfied. The next day I would come back with the full fro again and he would wonder, how in the world did that happen. It was OK with me because I got a chance to leave school a lot because of that. They never figured out how our hair works!"

I was standing at the door where I was assigned as an usher in my church looking out the glass window with another usher. We talked about our hair and the drama of having hair. I do not remember if the other usher was white or black since we all have issues with our hair. After she left to do something, I heard the Holy Spirit say, "Wear your hair like the little girls do with beads. But wear black beads and not all the multicolored ones." I thought what a cool idea. My best friend, Debra, put my hair in various styles. Most of the hair was corn rolled into whatever curves or straight lines that Debra wanted. I let her pick the style of the month. Each braid was closed by black beads and rubber bands. "Clank clank!" the beads sounded when I walked. I loved this style, especially when it was different every month, and so maintenance-free. All I had to do was wash it and the style was still there. No shrinkage, no patting, no picking. I might have wrapped it in a silk scarf at night, but nothing else was necessary. I wore this style for several years until my girlfriend moved to California and I had to find someone else to do it.

"You need to wear a hair style that becomes your age!" someone told me about my beaded hair.

"I like it like this!" I pouted.

"Well, that's on you!"

I continued to wear that style for a while but kept hearing this in my head. It was time for another change. On occasion if traveling on a cruise or to a hot place I would have someone braid my hair and add extensions to last for months. Buying hair and adding it to mine was costly and took hours to braid. It always amazed me how strong braiders' hands were and how long they could braid. Once braided it was easy maintenance, wash and go. I liked that style, but when my hair grew, you could see where my hair ended, and the extension started. It took hours on my part to take that hair down before going back for a rebraid; plus, I had to wash it too. Most braiders expected you to walk in with a fro ready for braiding. It was worth the effort to unbraid and wash, but again sucked up time out of life.

One thing I did enjoy about having extensions in my hair, I could wear my hair down my back. I longed for long hair and it seemed that was never going to happen. The longest it ever got was to the top of my shoulders. It grew and somehow would break off after a time.

Eventually I went back to flat ironing it. I returned to a salon because my cousin, Melanie had a shop. Unlike other salons I did not have to wait forever to get my hair done. She flat ironed and curled my hair in whatever style I asked. It was simply great getting to know her better and talk with her regularly. She was younger than I. Because of our age difference we knew each other but did not hang out. This was a perfect fit for me to know her as family. We laughed and cried about all kinds of life issues.

"Girl, you need to have a hair style that works with your natural curl pattern!" she piped in one day.

Curl pattern?

"Everyone's hair curls a certain way. Yours would look even more beautiful allowing that pattern to come through."

"What does that mean?" I asked.

"It would be more natural. I would put certain products in your hair, and it would just flow with your curl pattern. No more press and curl. Since it is summer, this is a perfect time to do this especially if you sweat a lot. Then when it gets cold again, we can go back to press and curl."

It took me a few weeks to decide, but I allowed her to wash my hair and put products in it. I walked out with a short wavy do. Wearing it naturally meant it was shorter than the straight flat iron look I was wearing. I loved it! It was summer, it kept my head cool and no worry about shrinkage in the rain or fog; water enhanced the look. I posted this look on Facebook and got tons of positive responses. When it got cooler, I kept it natural; this was the way to go.

Sometime during that year, I went to a party about natural hair. It was a fun party of African American women sharing their stories about their natural hair journey. They talked of products and who did their hair. It helped me to understand that a flat iron style is a natural hairstyle even though the heat changes the shape of the curl pattern to straight. This party encouraged me not to return to flat iron even more. What I was wearing was simple and the natural curl pattern God gave me shone through. It also made me realize as a race we *did* have "naturally curly" hair like white women did, just different. As a race, African Americans have been deceived into thinking our hair is ugly and should look like a white person's, long and straight. I found out later from interaction with white women how they agonize over their too curly hair or whatever it was they did not like about their hair. Media imposed on all of us what the acceptable image should be and we swallowed it hook, line and sinker.

At this party, I met Avis. Listening to her story as a natural hair stylist and wearer warmed my soul. She was what I needed. Her long medium-sized dreadlocks longs hang down her back in waves. I loved hers, but I did not want dreadlocks. Something about them on me, just did not work for me. Once I saw a woman with dreadlocks, I was appalled. They looked so unkept and dirty. It reminded me of how they portray Africans – wild, dirty, uneducated and savages. I was an American, not a wild African! Plus, I loved to change my hairstyle often. If I had dreadlocks I would have been bound into that style, never able to change my hairstyle. To stop having dreadlocks meant cutting them off and starting over with nearly a fuzz of hair from what I saw. I was not ready for that type of commitment.

Sometime later, I landed in Avis' chair. She worked out of her home. She washed and dried my hair and continued to style it with my natural curl pattern as my cousin had done. She put it in all kinds of styles with braids, corn rolls and twists. I allowed her to come up with any style, like I did when Debra did my hair, unless I needed a particular style for an event. Every time I sat in her chair; I admired her hair. More of her journey came through in that chair. Every time I saw her, her locs were in a different style, up, down, curly, wavy, braided, pulled back, knotted and more. I learned wearing locs would enable me to change up my hair style and not be stuck with one style like I feared. I just would not be able to have it flat, straight and shiny, like I sometimes like to have it.

The more I saw her hair, the more I wanted that style. She encouraged me to try twists first to see how it feels and looks then I would take it down before it started to lock and wore a natural wave pattern style I created at home. Twists were wonderful. My hair was short but beautiful, light and fashionable. She styled it in various ways. There was never a style I did not like. Soon I got to a point, I did not want to take the hair down, especially if I allowed it to be twisted too long and it was starting to lock. Detangling the style some-times was a chore. I was ready to have "locs" (short for dreadlocks). The word "dread" has a negative connotation to the style.

"Are you sure you want to do that?" My husband asked.

"Yes, hopefully it will grow long, and it will be so much easier to manage."

"What if you want to change your hair style? You always like doing that."

"Then I will cut it out, but I don't see that hap-pening for some reason. I think I will like locs forever."

"I don't know if I can get used to that look. But if it is something you want to do, do it." Dan had always been supportive of what crazy ideas I chose. This was the first time, he hedged. I prayed this would not be a problem later.

"Let me remind you, you will probably go through an 'ugly' stage while your hair changes from what you have now to being locked," Avis warned me. She and others had told me the early stages of making this change sometimes did not look so pretty, with hair sticking all over the place. I was ready for that "ugly" stage and using her look as a vision of what might come after that. I just hoped I could deal with being in public and with my husband while being "ugly."

My last set of twists occurred on October 2, 2013. I posted an "Operations Loc" Album on Facebook. My plan was to journalize this journey and note the changes that occur. Those twists locked in about a month, shorter than thought. Not having to take them down was a thrill. I had monthly meetings with Avis as the twists transformed into locs. My first cruise occurred the following month; it was freeing to have a minimal maintenance hairstyle while on vacation. It was wrapped in a silk scarf every night like I did when it was in twists to keep the style in place. Only Avis could wash it in the early days so that it would not untwist if I washed it. This meant I could not swim for a few weeks. I was good with that. It did not take long before I was able to wash it and swim. My hair length in twists barely reached my ears. With the flat iron it touched my shoulders. I hoped it would grow.

I waited and waited for the "ugly" stage to come. As time progressed my hair looked more beautiful. Avis waited too. That "ugly" stage never came.

"It might be because when you started your locs your hair had some length. Most people start their locs when their hair is short, so the hair looks crazy while it is transforming. What a blessing this never happened with you," Avis explained.

"God is with me," I confirmed. I thank God I did not deal with the "ugly" stage. I guess he knew it would be more than I could bear or that my husband would hate it. It grew faster than either of us could have dreamed. I took pictures every few months to show the changing texture and length. Some of those pictures I posted on Facebook, but most I kept for my own records. It has been six going on seven years since I started this journey. My locs are in the middle of my back. I love the freedom of having it in many styles from curly to straight, with such easy care, wash, dry and a special oil of Avis' creation in it. It seems everyone's hair Avis touches grows like it has never grown before. All the products she uses is natural and created by her or are natural purchases. I use a shampoo I can only buy at Trader Joes because it is natural.

To wear hair naturally like God intended has been a huge blessing for me. My hair has never been this long before. God granted my heart's desire for long hair. I am now sixty-four years old with long hair. It is not falling out like we are told should happen when you grow older. My hair is thick and healthy. If it were possible to unlock all this hair, I can imagine it would be past my butt. But that is not possible to learn.

"Now I am trying to figure out how long do I want these locs. They seem to be growing with no end. I don't want them dragging on the floor or below my butt," I said to Danielle, from my church.

"When your locs hit the toilet seat, when you are using the bathroom, it is time for a cut!" she told me. Her locs are thick and down to her waist, just like another sister in our church. I have been eyeing their locs for years. I have also been eyeing Debra's, my best friend who moved to California. She and I look like sisters. She started her locs years before I was ready, but I admired how they look on her. I often said if I had started at the same time as she they would have been longer earlier. But I also know it was not yet God's timing for me in my journey; I had to meet Avis. I have heard and seen too many horror stories of locticians who have ruined men and women's hair and caused balding. I did not want that. Long locs with bald foreheads is not attractive. With Avis, a guy with a bald forehead grew his hair back.

God also sent me to her because we talk about God and what he is doing in our lives while I sit in the chair. I love hearing about where God has sent her and what happened there and her future visions of His return.

Year five with locs has shown me, the locs are at the length I want them to be forever. I do not want them down to my waist. That is way too much hair to wash and style. Halfway down my back is perfect. So, Avis cuts it when it gets too long. I can style it, wash it and do whatever I want with it. I thank God for what he has done with my hair. It is amazing how much less I look at myself in the mirror. Sometimes I forget in the morning when I walk out the door. Unless I need to put it in a special style where I need the mirror, I only give it a glance before I leave. With my other styles I lived in front of the mirror; it had to be perfect, not a hair out of place. Even when there is a loc out of place, it's all good. I cannot explain it. It is almost like I do not care what I look like because I look good no matter what. I also ask God to remove any vanity that might creep into my thoughts because it is only because of Him that this hair exists on my head. When I do look at myself, I am amazed it is me with long hair.

Thanks to God, I can wear His hair as He meant for me to wear it, without any insecurities about how I look to man. Each day it looks different, just because of how it fell or was styled. Each day it is lovely in His sight. That is all that matters. His creation, worn His way.

CHAPTER FOURTEEN

THE WEIGHT WATCHER

*"For you created my inmost being;
you knit me together in my mother's womb.
I praise you because I am fearfully and
wonderfully made;
your works are wonderful,
I know that full well."
Psalm 139:13-14.*

I was always small as far as I was concerned and did not have a weight problem. In high school I ran track and walked everywhere. As a non-driving adult, I walked and took the bus where I needed to go. After learning to drive, I was physically active with camping, backpacking, hiking, walking, swimming and scuba diving. Being active was and still is what I do.

"Look at this chart!" My doctor pointed to the white computer screen, eyes wide, lips in a tight line. "Over the past five years your weight has gone up. It is now 199 pounds. Something is not right with that. You need to lose some weight!"

What? How could that be? 200 pounds was calling my name – no way! *Yeah, I knew I was heavier than in high school, but who stays the same size they were when they were kids? Yeah, I noticed there was a little meat in my hips, but that is just a sign of maturity as an older woman. Yeah, my bra size had gotten larger, but after kids that just happens. Besides it's nice having a little more up there to show off,* my old way of thinking crept in.

Two hundred pounds almost?! That is WAY too much! How could I have let this happen? My husband and I eat right. Because of his health issues he stays away from pork and red meat; chicken and fish are his choices. I eat meat of all kinds. So why the steady climb in weight? I am moving my body all over the place!

I did not consider myself an emotional eater. But I must have been a little bit. Over that five-year period, I did go through an emotional rough point in our marriage. I do not recall doing it, but I must have been eating. I know I was not happy, and I felt unloved, unwanted and unappreciated. Thus, I did not care what I looked like in public. Pictures of me in an orange and black flowered silky top and pants outfit I loved from Jamaica showed how full I really was. The thick meat on my elbow disgusted me. The thick neck and full face smiled at me. I was *that* girl; "she is fat but has a pretty face". Arrggh!

Immediately I went into action. I cut down my food consumption. *That's it!* I was active but eating more than I was burning – simple as that! I reduced my portion sizes, but found I was hungry a lot, so that did not last long. I needed a *real* plan! With a million and one diet plans out there, which one was for real? Plus, I didn't have a lot of money to pay for any of them. Thanks to God, Weight Watchers came to my government workplace. It was for a twelve-week session that was payable in full when you signed up. When I saw the price, I tossed that idea in the trash; I did not have the money.

"Check with your insurance company; maybe they offer something. Weight Watchers is partnered with many insurance companies," the coworker who was coordinating this session told me.

Yeah right, I thought. I checked with my insurance company. They reimbursed half of whatever I paid up to a certain dollar amount for programs such as Weight Watchers. I scrounged up some money and paid, knowing I would get half of it back.

"Little bear here says it is important that you get your fruits, vegetables, water, fiber and protein in every day for successful weight loss." Colleen, our leader darted around the room, perky, smiley, yet genuine as she spoke about that week's topic. It was week one.

I want to be like her! I thought. *That looks like so much fun being a Weight Watcher Leader. I love working with props and speaking publicly. When I lose this weight, I will do the same thing she is doing.*

Changes in portion size, preparation, meal planning and intended activity occurred during those twelve weeks. Each day I had to have five servings of fruits and vegetables, two servings of milk, some healthy oil (olive, canola, safflower, sunflower or flaxseed) and six glasses of water. Due to my age, weight and sex it was calculated that my daily allowance was twenty-three points for eating. Thirty-five additional points could be used anytime during the week. I weighed in at 191.4 pounds. I marked all our packaged products in our house with the appropriate point value. Every lick and bite were recorded in my three-month journal. I lost 4.8 pounds the first week mainly due to water.

I started this journey on November 18, 2008, just before Thanksgiving. With Thanksgiving and Christmas looming before me I wondered how this was going to work. "Next week I commit to: lose one to two pounds at least not gain since it's Thanksgiving," I wrote in my three-month journal. The Tuesday and Wednesday before Thanksgiving I ate within my twenty-three daily points. I did not want to go over and use any of my thirty-five allowance points for the week. I saved those thirty-five points for Thanksgiving to add to my twenty-three daily points.

Thanksgiving was at our home. Others brought food, but we had control of the main course; I needed control this year.

"Just take a small sample of those things you normally don't get to eat until you are satisfied, not full." Colleen's voice rang in my ear. I did just that. My plate was full of the small portions of turkey, peas, mashed potatoes, roll, gravy, cranberry sauce, mac and cheese, cornbread stuffing, chocolate cake with white icing along with a glass of punch. It tasted so good as I savored each bite. I sat for a moment when the plastic plate was clean. I was not hungry. There was plenty more food. Normally I run back for seconds. Having *one* roll was unheard of for me; I *love* bread! I was surprised to see I really was satisfied as Colleen warned me to be, not full. Full belly pressing against tight buttons/zippers and the need to lay down and rest was my mode of operation. *This* felt good, no pain from being full and I was energized! Food is supposed to *give* energy, not *sap* energy. My eyes gazed at everyone else; they were all zapped out and lounging on couches. I smiled as I scurried to clean dishes and put food away.

That day I started with fifty-eight points (twenty-three daily points plus thirty-five weekly allowance points). After two meals of breakfast and supper I ended the day with twelve points. Wooo whooo! I had twelve points I could carry over to be used on a day later in the week! I also did forty-five minutes of cleaning the house and cooking to gain three points of activity. I am sure it was more than forty-five minutes, but I wanted to be conservative on how much activity I did. Without those three extra points my balance would have been nine. Either way I had those weekly allowance points for later in the week.

"Since Thanksgiving was so successful, Christmas is going to be a piece of cake!" I told my husband. I was eager for the challenge. By the Tuesday after Thanksgiving, I had lost 4.2 pounds!

After two successful weeks, my new life began. Each day I did twenty to fifty minutes of some sort of activity, walking or riding a stationary bike. This was easy-peasy!

Christmas was the least of my concerns; I had to get through a cruise before Christmas. "You should have waited until after Thanksgiving, your cruise and Christmas to go on a diet. That is the worst time to start," someone not on a diet told me.

"I didn't have a choice, the twelve-week session started the week before Thanksgiving; I didn't want to wait."

On December 10, 2008, Dan, me and a group of friends from church and high school flew to Fort Lauderdale to meet our cruise ship. With three-month journal in hand, I wrote, "I commit to: no weight gain on cruise! Do two activity points a day." Everyone in our group knew I was on a diet.

"I am watching you!" one of my church members said loudly. She has a way of saying things that irritate me, but this time I did not let it bother me. It was a five-day cruise; everyone was watching my plate. Each day was Thanksgiving for me, except I ramped up my activity. I love cruises! With cruises activity is the easiest thing to do. You must walk to and from all your meals. Dan and I always take the stairs instead of the elevators. The outdoor track was my best friend; Dan joined me. We snorkeled in choppy water – that was a workout! We walked on land. I ate all my daily, weekly and activity points; I left no un-eaten point behind! I lost 5.6 pounds!!

"Congratulations!" Colleen handed me a yellow five-pound star and a green bravo sticker for sharing my story.

"How did you do that!" one of my coworkers asked. "I just knew you were going to come back with a huge weight gain. It is soooo hard to lose weight while on a cruise."

"It was easier than I thought; I just followed the plan. I didn't deny myself anything. I just didn't eat a thousand pounds of food like I normally do."

Losing weight was my goal, but my real goal was to become a Weight Watcher Leader, so I could be just like Colleen excited about sharing her success.

During the remaining weeks of the twelve-week session, an average of two pounds a week was lost. One week I only lost .2 pounds one week but gained .8 pounds another week. By the end of the session I had lost 26.8 pounds. I passed my 10% target goal loss and was ready to finish this party!

"Unfortunately, we don't have enough people to have another session!" Colleen told those of us who had showed up for another session. There had to be a minimum number of people for each session and this time, our group was not large enough.

"No way! I gotta keep going. I am still so far away from where I need to be!" I groaned.

"You can attend other meetings we have in the community," Colleen encouraged us.

"That means I have to go before or after work. This location is so convenient."

"We have a location right next door in the Crowne Center at about this same time. Maybe that can work for you. You can walk over there."

"Thanks!" I was there!

"Welcome to Weight Watchers!" the tall, lean, brown-skinned leader shook my hand. I had to keep my mouth from dropping – someone who look like me! I thanked God for sending me to this place that was next door to where I work, where I could go during my lunch hour. Seeing an African American was the most encouraging. I already knew from my first twelve-weeks that I could lose weight even as an African American, but seeing this shapely, energetic and informative leader gave me hope that I could keep it off as an African American.

"Those BMI numbers are for white girls!" I told Trudy, the leader. "I put down 150 pounds as my goal weight with Colleen which is the top of the BMI. I have never been that small before. So, I will have to wait to see what that looks like when I get there."

"Yes, you will have to wait and see. You might be pleasantly surprised. I thought the same thing when I was losing weight." She smiled.

Thus, my journey continued with Trudy as my leader.

"Whoop! Whoop!" Trudy fist pumped! "Juel reached her goal weight. How many pounds did you lose? Tell us how you did it!"

"I lost 41 pounds. I focused on making sure I tracked everything I ate and ate all the healthy guideline foods for the day. Tracking, however, was key," I answered after being awarded my Goal Reacher Award.

"Now, Juel has to show for the next six weeks that she can maintain that weight. Once she shows that she can maintain her goal weight, then she will become a Lifetime member and no longer pay. As a lifetime member, she will weigh in once a month, to show that she is maintaining her goal weight. Congratulations, Juel!"

Losing the weight was easy. Maintaining was another story. My goal weight was one hundred and fifty pounds. Just as Trudy had told me I was pleasantly surprised that one hundred and fifty pounds looked good on me; I was not skinny as I feared. During those six weeks I had to adjust my eating habits. I had my daily point value increased; I had to eat more. My body was conditioned to losing and it was not ready to stop. I lost another 7.2 pounds in those six weeks. Only one of those weeks I did not lose.

"Celebration Time! Juel is now a Lifetime Member!" Applause, cheers, sharing and receipt of my Lifetime Key. I was now 142.4 pounds – total loss 48.2 pounds. At this weight, I looked good, was even more energetic and fit a size six to eight depending on the manufacturer.

"What are you doing?" I jumped up from my pillow as Dan leaned over me.

"Watching you breathe," he said.

"What?"

"You are not snoring. Most nights you snore my ear off and I can't sleep. Now you are not snoring anymore. I have been watching you for several nights to be sure. It has to be the weight loss – no more weight in your neck."

No wonder I was sleeping better; my husband was not knocking me awake to stop the snoring. My mild case of sleep apnea was no more – a weight loss benefit I was not planning on.

When I originally started this trek, my goal was to lose forty pounds within a year. Instead I lost 48.2 pounds in six months. Sticking to the plan really worked! All during that time I had gains, losses and maintenance, but it worked. There was a plateau that was reached where no loss occurred. A discussion with my leader revealed I was not getting enough dairy and healthy oil in. Once I consumed the daily requirement, the weight flew off.

Weight continued to leave my body after reaching goal weight. It was hard! Eating more to make the body stop was hard! In my eyes I still looked good. I had never been at this size before and I was loving it! I had to pray, pray, and pray that the nonverbals and catcalls from guys would not make me vain, as I relished the attention. That was even harder, remembering that God was my husband and His love is all that I needed. Plus,

God gave me an earthly husband, so I need not savor over being attractive by other men. My lowest weight was one hundred and thirty-seven pounds – a total of fifty-three pounds in the same year that I turned fifty-three years old. At fifty-three I had more energy than I did when I was a teenager. Crazy! That fact about getting older and losing your metabolism is not true if you are active and have a healthy eating lifestyle.

"Girl, you need to stop losing weight."

"Are you ok?"

"Are you sure you are not sick?"

"Girl, you look like a rail. You need to stop!"

"You look sickly. You face is sunken in. Stop!"

I shucked off the naysayers. In my mind they were just jealous of how good I looked and that I had really lost the weight. I know they were waiting for me to gain it all back, but that was not going to happen. I did not do all this work to go back to that depressed, unhappy, overweight woman; she was dead!

"What is this on my hand?" I asked my doctor, the one who told me I needed to lose weight.

"It is called your joint. You are so small now you can see your joints. See you can feel your rib cage and the sternum. You have lost too much weight!"

"Not so! I am good!" I left out of there with pouting lips. *How dare she tell me I lost too much weight. It's her fault I lost the weight. She is just jealous because she is obese and one of her patients took her advice and did it! She is the one that needs to be losing the weight!*

Pictures tell a thousand stories. I looked at a family reunion picture of me in a flowery sun dress. I looked like a starving person without the big belly. *What????* I could see my collar bones, ribs and most of my bones. It was not like I looked like a skeleton with skin on, but it was getting close. I also noticed that sitting down for long periods of time was uncomfortable. I had lost my cushion in my buttocks to sit on. I sat on bone. Then I lost my breast. I was a lean mean fighting machine. Since I had already had a hysterectomy, I did not get a chance to notice if my periods had stopped because of being so lean. With that picture, I knew this *had* to stop! I *had* to seriously have a plan to eat back some of that weight I lost and to do some weight resistance to ton up that flesh. Eating more and weight training toned me up. My breast and buttocks increased to a size I preferred. I wanted to be small, but I wanted to have a shape that was pleasing to my husband's eye. I gained weight to maintain between one hundred and forty-two and one hundred and forty-five pounds, which is where I stay to this date. Anything lower than one hundred and forty pounds does not look good on me.

With weight loss/gain behind me, the next chapter began – being a Weight Watcher Leader.

At the age of fifty-three, I was starting over – at the bottom of the ladder. It was my first real corporation job. My employment experiences had been with three government agencies. I continued to work full time with the Internal Revenue Service, as I worked part time for Weight Watchers. Before I could become a Leader, I had to work as a receptionist. The receptionist greets members and weighed them in. This one-on-one encounter with regular and new members was key in being a source of encouragement. After a certain period and training, I was advanced into the role of a Weight Watcher Leader.

"I learn more as a leader/teacher than I do as a student," I told one of my coworkers. "As a leader/teacher I really come to grips with whether or not I really know my stuff."

"I know what you mean. When I was losing the weight, I thought one way. Once I lost it and began to share that experience with others is when I learned, the why's and how's and if I really lost it the right way," she said.

"Right, the truth comes out." I laughed. "I have had to tweak my method of maintenance to make sure I am setting the proper example for the members by how I live this lifestyle. I never stop learning, even as a leader."

This was a job I loved! I loved it because it was not a job; it was a passion! I told myself if it ever became a job, it was time to leave. I had a job; I did not need a second job. I saw myself doing this forever. Standing in front of people delivering the weekly topic for the week, personally encouraging members, cheering on members, comforting them and telling my success story was fun. Using props, flip charts, videos, audio and any other type of aids was my favorite thing to do. Engaging members in the meetings was what I tried to do. I tried to be the leader that kept members alert and assisted them in their journey, like I had been. I pray that is what I was for many and that I was a positive impact for many.

After five years in this role, God made it clear, it was time to move. Nothing lasts forever. From past experiences I had learned the consequences of not listening and obeying God's call to close one door to open another one; I knew this door had to be closed immediately.

I remained a Weight Watcher member after I left the payroll. This lifestyle is the best out there and I continue to weigh in once a month as a lifetime member. Once a month I dine with former coworkers who still work there or are also former employees. The relationships gained while a member and employee are deep. I thank God for taking me down this path of being overweight so that I can have these relationships and be a source of help for others. The paths God leads us down are for us and the benefit of others.

"Why can't that person lose weight? If they would simply push themselves away from the table, then maybe they wouldn't be the size they are. So, they need to stop complaining and just do it!" This is what I used to say to myself before God allowed me to lose my sight and pack on a few pounds myself. Now I understand and can relate.

As a Leader, God enabled me to further understand the why's of weight gain from the physical to the mental in the members and in myself. I carry a "before" picture of me and show it whenever the talk of weight comes up with others.

"That doesn't even look like you. You look so much older." I hear all the time.

"Yeah, weight ages you. I am not going back to that girl ever again. She was not happy, and her weight showed it. She had a low self-esteem even though you couldn't tell it." My outside mantra was "Wear a smile and carry a positive attitude." My inside mantra was "I am not loved and unhappy." Keeping this before picture close is for me and others. It is a reminder of where God has taken me and not to look back on the good old days as good. They were not always so.

God's goodness and purpose lights my path of healthy living to share with others, so they can become the best temple for God. If it were not for Him taking me from that path of destruction, no telling where I would be overweight, unhappy, with knee and back pain, sleep apnea, diabetes, high blood pressure and more. With Him, I am lighter than I was in high school, healthier, joyful and able to do His will as His wonderfully made creation.

CHAPTER FIFTEEN

THE HUMBLED WALKER

*"Now I, Nebuchadnezzar, praise and exalt
and glorify the King of heaven, because everything he does is right and all his ways are just.
And those who walk in pride he is able to
humble." Daniel 4:37.*

If someone told me I would pay cash money
to suffer by walking miles in one day for a medal
and T-Shirt I would have laughed in their face.
Why would I do that? Yet, I have done that very
thing – repeatedly.

Losing weight led me down this path. Changing my food choices was the start, and walking
enabled the weight to come off faster, toned the
muscles and kept the weight off. I have walked all
my life – to school, to play, to carry jugs of milk
from the store that I have dropped as a child, to
friends, to the bus, to work, to everywhere my par-
ents/husband did not take me in a car. Before I
learned to drive, my two feet were my mode of
transportation.

My stride was long and fast because of my dad. He was a letter carrier. As a little girl I had to walk fast with my shorter legs to keep up to his pace. He walked a lot and the muscles in his legs showed it. I wonder how many miles a day he walked carrying mail from house to house.

"Slow it down! I can't keep up!" People tell me when I walk with them, even when I am walking slowly. Walking slow, too slow, is painful!

"Walking is something you can do anywhere you go! You don't need any special equipment, except a good pair of walking shoes," one of my Weight Watcher leaders told us in one of the meetings. "If you are going to do a race or any long distances you will need some special wicking clothes that wicks off your sweat, but other than that, you are good to go anywhere anytime. We all have feet, use them."

So, I did. I walked at least three times a week with three different friends while losing the weight. I had to walk more than I did regularly in a day for it to be effective for weight loss. These early walks were short half hour to an hour walks around an indoor track at my local recreation center. It was winter, so walking outside was not a consideration. Round and round we went laughing and talking about whatever. Walking with someone made it easier to walk the time away on that track. It was downright boring when I walked by myself. I tried wearing earplugs for music when I was alone. Sometimes that worked, but it never quite took for me. Wearing the plugs and carrying the phone was a pain for me. I did not understand how people did it, holding a phone and walking at the same time. There were other devices I saw that did not require carrying a phone, but none of them interested me either. I wanted to hear whatever sounds were going on around me and not be cocooned in music. Walking then was merely a means to lose to weight and hang out with my girlfriends and nothing else.

"How do they do it?" I asked my husband, while we were watching *Biggest Loser* on television. "Those guys are still tons overweight, yet they are running marathons."

"Size has nothing to do with doing or not doing a marathon. Anyone can if they train," Dan said. "Plus, you see how long some of them took to finish - hours. They didn't run the entire time, sometimes they walked."

"Still, that seems like a lot of weight to be lugging for 26.2 miles. Here I have lost the weight and I am not doing any marathons. I should be able to do the same thing they are doing."

"Sure, you can, just do it." I thought about it and filed it away in the back of my mind. I had no real reason to run a marathon. I was no longer heavy; I walked just to keep it off along with walking on an elliptical on my job. Lifting weights or anything "gym" related was a turn off for me. Walking with friends on tracks and outside was fun. That other stuff like weights and exercise was work! Not to mention, there was a cost to be part of a "gym" I did not want to pay because I knew I would not go enough to cover what I paid. I also did not like others watching me while I worked out; that was uncomfortable.

Week after week I watched the *Biggest Loser.* Watching TV is not what I do, there is no time in my schedule to sit and just watch. However, this show caught my eye after Dan had watched it for a few years. The title was a turn-off for me the first few years, so I did not watch it. It sounded like a show about a bunch of losers on a reality show. Realty shows were a turn off for me to begin with. Once I realized their goal was to lose weight like I had lost, I watched it with my husband, instead of walking by and taking sneak peaks. Each year when the marathon part of the show came, I was intrigued, I wanted to do the same.

"What the heck do you think about when you are running a marathon? That is a lot of hours to be running. That sounds so boring, on and on. There has got to be a faster way to do a marathon," I said to Barb, a personal trainer friend of mine from church. She told me something to explain what she thought about in a marathon and that it was not so boring. I was not convinced.

"Is it really worth it? How in the world do people do that? They train and train and then they die falling across a finish line. Really? How can someone be so self-absorbed about winning a medal, that maybe their family will have in their memory. If it is not for the Olympics what is the big deal with doing so many races for a participant's medal that everyone gets. I mean, only the top three get any money," I ranted to someone, anyone, as I tried to convince myself these athletes were demon-possessed.

Watching those "biggest losers" cross the finish line nagged at me. "I could do that and better! But I do not need to enter a race. That is crazy. Maybe I could just do those miles in a park and just be able to say I did 26.2 miles. That is all I want to do, to show I can do it. I do not need a medal. I am good," I remember telling somebody.

I started to run instead of walk on the track with no training plan. I did not have anyone to run with, except Dan and Maggie, a girlfriend, who survived two bouts of breast cancer. Maggie was one of the three women who walked with me while losing the weight. She was the fastest of the three and dragged me along whether we were walking or running. She was fit! In spite of her chemo-thinned hair and neuropathy in her feet, it was hard keeping up with her. I wanted to be fit like her and healthy. She used to be a step and exercise instructor before cancer met her; she did not let cancer keep her from staying fit.

"Make sure you check your breast every month. If it weren't for that I would not have found both cancers early enough. The mammograms don't find them soon enough and insurance companies won't pay the cost of machines that will discover cancer sooner until cancer is suspected." I heard it from her and doctors, I knew I should, but I did not. I would start for a month a two, but then I would stop.

She and I walked and ran in parks and the indoor track. My knees hurt while trying to run. That did not happen when I walked.

"You need to exercise the muscles around your knees in order for them to get stronger, so you can run," Barb told me. "Start off by training for shorter races such as a 5K, 10K and a half marathon instead of training for a full right off the bat. That will also help in strengthening the muscles so that you will be ready for a full marathon."

She put me on a training regimen to do at home. This was exercise, but at the time it was worth it, so I could run. Exercising at home was worse than exercising at a gym to me; I was not thrilled to do it and I could easily talk myself out of not doing it. For my knees I did exercise for a longer time than I have ever done. Maybe also because I see Barb at church, and she gave me a level of accountability I could not get away from. My doctor also confirmed that physical therapy was what was needed for the knees to strengthen the muscles around them. So, between my doctor's instructions and Barb's I did at-home knee workouts.

As a teenager I ran track. I ran the 880-yard run and threw a shot put. Running as a woman in my fifties was different. Different in that besides the knee discomfort, it was boring as I ran in circles. As a more mature woman I had to intentionally put this marathon thing into a busy schedule. As a teenager, my schedule was busy, but seemed more fun.

"You need to just walk," Louis, a brother from church, told me, when I revealed I was planning to run a marathon in a park.

"Walk? That would take forever. Running a marathon is long enough."

"I walk all my marathons."

"How long does that take?"

"About five and a half hours."

"See, that is what I am talking about. That is a long time. What are you thinking about when you are out there that long?" Walking was not an option for me. *This dude is crazy! He can walk five and a half hours, but it will take me longer to walk a marathon. Boooring!*

"The time really goes fast. It's hard to explain. You get into a zone and get it done," he said.

"Ok, I will think about it, but I would rather run and get it over with." I walked off.

Thinking about doing a marathon and training for one was two different things. I worked full time for the government. I walked or ran with friends to stay in shape while pondering on how this marathon could happen. After looking at training plans, I knew I did not have time to train after work or on weekends. My days were always full of things to do, places to go. The dream was there; how it was to be fulfilled seemed remote.

"What do you want for your retirement celebration and gift?" one of my coworkers asked me.

"Just the ordinary gathering of family and friends in the office for lunch. Nothing special. I don't want to go out and make people pay for an expensive lunch/dinner. Anything that can be held within the office." I leaned back in my chair. It was hard to believe retirement was just around the corner. "As a gift? That's a good one. What I really need is money to buy shoes and workout clothes to train for a marathon after I retire."

"OK, we will work on that," this coworker said. As I type this it makes me think of her. She never made it to retirement. She died the year she was in the process of retiring, seven years after I retired. How precious life is and taken so for granted. She arranged my entire celebration and with her sister created a handmade shoe stuffed with money for clothes and shoes to do a marathon.

One Sunday, while I was ushering, I saw one of our members coming into service later than normal. He was dressed in a sweaty, reddish T-shirt and came straight to us as ushers to get his communion.

"Where are you coming from looking like that?" I asked Eric. He looked like he had just worked out.

"I just ran the Rite Aid Marathon. I didn't want to miss out on getting communion."

"Wow!" I saw that T-shirt and I wanted it! "Did you get a medal?"

"Sure did! It's in the car." Eric smiled, then slipped in the rear rows of the congregation, like he had been there all along. The medal was not what I coveted; I coveted that cool shirt with Rite

Aid Marathon plastered across the front. I signed up for the 2012 Rite Aid marathon right after church for the next year.

Retirement gave me the time to train. I trained to do smaller races. I learned soon that running was not an option for me. It did not feel right on my body. Walking is what I loved. Watching Louis helped me to see that it might take a little longer, but the body recovers quicker, and the distance is the same. So, I continued to walk with friends. Walking distances proved to be more challenging that walking a few miles around a track. I had to learn what foods and drinks worked for me to keep my energy up and prevent injury. At one point I was not sure if I could do this.

"How am I going to walk 26.2 miles, if I have to pee every 15 to 20 minutes?" I whined to Maggie on one of our walks.

"I don't know, you need to figure out what is going on. You should not have to go that often. That is crazy! Maybe you got some type of bladder thing going on or you are drinking too much."

I went to the doctor. Nothing was wrong with the kidneys or bladder. I was given a brochure on what to eat or drink if having issues with frequent urination. All the proper foods were what I was eating as a Weight Watcher member. Coffee was a key cause of diuretic and was told to avoid that. I hate coffee! It smells delicious, but the taste does not match; so, coffee was never my drink of choice. Then I noticed on the list that black tea and other teas were a high source of diuretic. I drank tea and hot chocolate every day!

Watermelon and other diuretic foods need to be avoided also. No wonder I had to go so much. Changing to herbal teas and not drinking or eating diuretic foods before going on a training walk eliminated the need to go to the bathroom so much. What a relief that was to be able to walk long distances and go on a more reasonable bathroom schedule. I find when there is a physical problem, diet is usually the culprit.

My first organized walks were short 5K's that supported some sort of cause. Our church walked an annual Walk 4 Hunger. No medals were involved in any of these walks, just fun times and raising funds for whatever the needs were for. The first 10K was also with the church for Lifebanc. This was my first medal.

"The last half of your race is faster than your first half," Sonny, our ministry leader told me on that race. I was the only one who did the 10K on August 13, 2011, the year I retired. The rest of the church did the 5K. He and his family stayed until I finished the race. Not only did he stay, but he ran back to find me and walked the rest of the race with me. This act of kindness and not leaving me behind warms me even now. Ending the race alone without someone at the end would have been a huge hurt for me. God made sure I was encouraged through His servant, Sonny.

The Towpath in the Cleveland Metroparks and Cuyahoga Valley National Park was where Maggie and I did our longest walks. It was flat and went on for miles. Maggie was my key source of inspiration as we walked miles on that Towpath. She walked with me with nails that turned black and fell off because of the distance and the neuropathy. Watching her suffer with me made me forget my soreness or tiredness as we walked.

Therefore, my first half marathon was the Towpath Half Marathon on October 9, 2011. This race started out in the pitch black and ended in the day. I walked it alone. I had gotten used to walking alone. God was always with me, so I really was not spiritually alone. It was just me and Him. I thanked God for giving me Maggie to train with; I do not know how I would have done that race without her there to train with. Dan and my father come to the race. However, they both missed seeing me cross the finish line. This race had two points of entering the finish line – one for the half marathoners and one for the full marathoners, Dan missed me while he was taking pictures of the full marathoners. My dad missed me but saw me at the last minute as I was crossing. So, there were no finish line shots taken by them from their cameras. Thank goodness I was able to buy professional finish line shots of me crossing the bridge to the finish line. That was a long race, but I loved every minute of it, even when muscles were ready to stop. In spite of aching muscles, bursts of energy drove me home. My last half of the race was stronger than my first half. I could barely walk to the car, but it felt good to have accomplished 13.1 miles.

Moving into a training plan for a marathon brought on more challenges – walking double-digit miles with someone. There was no one available to walk the long walks on weekends. Maggie could only walk so far with me. I was not comfortable walking alone in any park as a woman; it just was not safe. On my training plan I had to walk twenty miles on two of my Saturdays. How was I going to do that? God made a way.

"Girl, I am training to do the Rite Aid Half the same year you are doing the full. Maybe I could ride my bike while you walk alongside," Colleen said. She was my first Weight Watcher Leader.

"Excellent! You will have to ride slow since I will not be able to walk fast enough to keep up with you." I grinned. "Then maybe I can walk with you to help you train for your half."

As it turned out, we trained together on foot. I do not remember why we changed our plans about the bike, but Colleen walked the entire twenty miles with me. Just like Maggie she suffered by walking more than she needed to for the half, but it gave me a partner to walk on the Towpath to train for the full. She was limping by the time we finished that walk. For that second twenty miles I did not want her to suffer again and be over trained. God provided another way.

Since I have a track mentality, I treated this first marathon as I would have as a track runner, train the distance planning to run. I have not seen a training plan for a marathon that made you run/walk the full 26.2 miles. The longest I have seen may have been twenty-two to twenty-four miles but not 26.2. I could not understand that. How in the world do you know if you can complete 26.2 miles if you have only gone twenty to twenty-four miles in practice? I decided I needed to do a full marathon in practice before the real one. I choose to walk twenty-seven miles inside on my favorite local indoor track.

With a folding chair to hold all my water supplies, nourishment, course map and Q-Tips® to mark my laps, I began the indoor trek. Training for the Rite Aid Marathon meant a lot of walking indoors because the training session is in the winter. The race is in mid-May and twenty-one weeks of training is needed. In northern Ohio that meant January to March are indoor training months. April and May are generally good outdoor months but too close to the race. The twenty-mile walks are at least a month to six weeks before the race. The last six weeks before the race miles are tapered down. Too many miles too close to a race can cause one to be over trained and risk injury. Colleen and I were blessed with a good day to walk outside when we did the twenty miles on the Towpath.

It is hard to keep track of the miles while walking inside. With only ten fingers, keeping track of the laps becomes a chore. Barb suggested I used Q-tips® to mark my way. At every lap, I would throw down a Q-tip®. I counted them ahead of time. Fourteen laps equaled a mile. For the twenty-seven miles I had individual packets of fourteen Q-tips in five-mile packets. Those packets were in that folder chair I placed in one of the curves of the track along with water and nutrition bars. A map of the Rite Aid course was taped to the chair. As I walked round and round, I only stopped where there was a bathroom or nutrition stop on the course for water to use the bathroom. As I walked, I visualized what street I was walking down and what I saw. "I am walking down Carnegie Avenue now." No longer was I walking on a small black track with white lines, I was outside on a street heading to the finish line.

"What are doing up here? You have been up here for hours! You need to stop!" someone broke into my concentration.

"What?" I asked as I slowed but did not stop. "I am just walking like I normally do – training for my marathon."

"No, you have never been up here this long. You need to stop!" the woman cried, her face was so torn up, I thought she was ready to have a heart attack. I did not get it. I was a regular and never had this happen before and the track was still open. "I am just worried about you up here. You might hurt yourself."

"I am all good. Worst case scenario, if you see something happen on the camera, you can call 911." I panted as I passed by her as she stood with hands on her hips alongside the track.

"OK, I will be watching you," she said and left the track to return to her desk where the monitor for the camera on the track was.

Eight hours later, I limped down the stairs with my stuff to the desk where she sat.

"Wow, you were up there a long time. I am sorry I gave you such grief. I was worried you were going to pass out and die. There was a guy who was walking up there one time before and he fell out and died. I thought that was going to happen to you," she spit out before I had a chance to ask why she wanted me to stop earlier.

"Oh, I was wondering. I couldn't figure out why you were so upset with me. I never saw you like that before. Thanks for being concerned for me."

I was in so much pain after eight hours on my feet, walking in circles. I was glad I would never have to do that again. This marathon was a bucket list dream, a one-time event, just to say I could do a marathon. Once this training and the race were done, I was through with marathons; I would return to walking for fun and staying in shape. After those twenty-seven miles, I was ready to get this race over with even though it was still weeks away. I wished there were some way I could do this marathon without all these weeks of training and time taken out of my life; this was work!

Can I really do this? I have trained but walking twenty-seven miles on an inside track is not the same as walking with elevation changes, weather, various paved terrain and people. Would I get injured, fall, "hit the wall," get lost, get sick, cramp up, anything that would keep me from finishing? Dan drove me downtown. We had to be there in the wee hours of the morning before the roads closed for a 7 a.m. start. The traffic was sluggish. We crept down East Ninth Street towards the Start Line at The Cleveland Browns Stadium on West Third. Our plan was to park near there.

"This is going really slow. I need to have enough time to pee before we start." I gazed out at the car traffic and the people walking down Ninth Street with bibs on heading to the Start Line. "This is taking forever."

"Take it easy. We will get there." Dan reached over and grabbed my hand.

"We are just sitting here. The race starts in about an hour and I don't know where the bathrooms are. The lines will be long; that could take forever. I need to get out and walk. You can meet me at the Start Line after you park," I rambled.

"OK, but I still think you have plenty of time," Dan tried to reassure me.

No, matter what he said, I was not having it. I jumped out of the van and walked about half a mile to get in line for the bathroom and then walked over to the rear of the Start Line. Finding me was not supposed to be difficult. As a walker we were the last in the pack at the Start Line. The faster runners and walkers lined up near the front. All are assigned to corrals that are based on the runner/walkers anticipated finish time. So, all Dan had to do was go to the end of the Start Line and look for me in the mob of people. This was my largest race and there were a lot of people, more than I anticipated. He had to use his cell phone to find me.

While I waited, I ran into Colleen my Weight Watcher Leader who was run/walking the half. She still had a limp from the training but was going to do this race anyway. She had some sort of joint pain that was going to have to be looked at later by a doctor. I am thinking it was her knee, a bone on bone thing. She did not want it to be treated before the race. She was ready to grin and bear it. People like her amaze me; I do not think I could do that if I were in the amount of pain her face told me. The plan was for us to start together, but then do our own race pace, especially since she was doing the half and I the full.

"Is this your first half?" I asked a person that I randomly started a conversation with.

"Yes, is this your first full?" she answered.

"Sure is." I smiled.

"This is my first half also." Another person next to us added in.

"Where are you guys from?" I asked them.

"Hubbard."

"Chicago."

"What? Chicago? You came all the way here to do a half marathon? You couldn't have picked a closer place?"

"No, this is the one I wanted to do, since it is fast, flat and has a long course time. I am walking this race," the woman from Chicago explained.

"I am walking too." Hubbard's grin spread across her face.

"Me too!" I said. "Where is Hubbard?"

"Near Youngstown."

"Oh, at least you didn't have as far to come. My name is Juel. What is yours?"

"Beth," Hubbard said.

"Theresa," Chicago responded.

"This here is my Weight Watcher Leader Colleen. She trained with me to get here." I pointed to Colleen who was standing there with another Weight Watcher member.

"Wow! I lost one hundred pounds on Weight Watchers!" Beth practically shouted.

"I lost weight on Weight Watchers too!" Theresa said.

The three of us laughed. Among thousands of people three people who lost weight on Weight Watchers found each other at a race that was their first in that category.

"Here is my husband, Dan. Dan, meet my new friends Beth and Theresa. This is Colleen the leader I told you about who trained with me. Quick take a picture of us, it is getting ready to start."

The three of us have been friends ever since. We had just enough time to make friends on Facebook so I could tag them after the picture was posted. Thank goodness we had the time to find each other on Facebook because once the race started, we never found each other again since Colleen, Beth and Theresa finished hours before I did. Our communication was through Facebook and phone. I could not believe I made friends with two strangers who were not of my race on the spot. There was something comforting about the two of them that made me exchange information with them on May 20, 2012. There were two other women there who were doing their first half. The five of us took a group shot together as virgin half and full marathon walkers. I do not remember their names; I think they were friends of Colleen. In any case no Facebook or phone number information was exchanged with them. God meant for me to know Beth and Theresa, not the other two.

Hot! Hot! Hot was this race! "Make sure you carry your own water, because there is always a chance that there will not be water when you want it," some wise person told me. In a fanny pack I carried extra water and nutrition bars. As a walker, water stations and support tend to thin out because it takes us longer to get to them than runners. The race started out cold because it was early in the day by Lake Erie. I wore long, black wicking pants and a long-sleeved gray wicking shirt under my neon green Rite Aid race shirt. I was planning to remove the long-sleeved shirt and pants when it got hot. I never did. The further I went the more I realized how those sleeves and pants protected me from the sun.

A few miles before the half a woman joined me. She had trained to run the full marathon, but did not fully get the miles in. She was told she could walk the marathon and still finish. She saw my pace and caught up with me. We walked and talked for a while. Soon it was obvious that the heat and the lack of getting the training miles in was not going to enable her to finish. Thanks to God someone with communication with medic was able to gather her and take her to help. She and I had exchanged Facebook information before we separated. I wanted to make sure she made it back safe and was well. I continued the rest of the race alone in the heat.

Little did I know that the race had turned to a black flag behind me. A black flag meant the race was stopped because of health hazard to participants, extreme heat in this case. Anyone behind me was being pulled from the race. I would have been crushed if I had gotten pulled. This was a bucket list race and I had no plans to do this again.

I was in pain; I was a woman walking alone in neighborhoods that I would not have walked alone in. I prayed for safety to get to the finish. Once while I was walking on Liberty Boulevard around mile twenty, I saw a guy coming down some stairs to where I was. I knew if he was going to try something it was going to be ugly because I was not at my best; I was ready to be done. Then, a medic truck drove up behind me; that person went back up the stairs to the street above. I thanked God, for I have no idea if that was something about to happen or not; it did not feel or look right. I was safe and moved on.

I waited to hit this "wall" walkers and runners talked about. It never came; I do not know what that means. What wall? All I know is that my pace got faster the closer I got to the finish line. I was not at the pace I had wanted to be at by the end, because of walking with the new friend that had to be pulled from the race. I just wanted to finish within the time limit mandated. The time spent with my new friend was worth the delay.

God probably needed me to slow down because it was too hot to walk too fast. God knows best. While I walked, I could hear when Louis from church reached certain markers in front of me; I was tracking him. I cheered him on while I sped along miles behind him. I was wishing I were up there with him, so much closer to the end of this walk. *Why was I doing this again? This hurt!*

"It's you and me God, just you and me. Let's get this done!" I chanted over and over. One foot in front of the other.

Somewhere close to mile twenty-six a guy cheering us on, cried out – "You are a marathoner!" Tears streamed down my face as I sped through those last few yards to the finish line. *A marathoner?* I never thought of myself becoming that by doing this, I just wanted to do it.

I saw the finish line looming before me. A guy with a microphone welcomed people across the line and announced their names. He saw me coming. "Here is someone coming who is walking in strong and despite the heat is wearing long sleeves and pants. Juel Fitzgerald from North Randall." Then he went on the say that wearing long sleeves and pants provides protection from the sun.

I hit my watch; it was done! I was a marathoner! A huge medal was put on my neck. I grabbed bananas, chips, pretzels, water, Gatorade, and chocolate milk as I looked for Danny. I walked slowly, after stretching, through the finish line area that leads back to the outside world. Professional pictures with my medal were posed for through that maze on the way out. I wondered how soon Theresa, Beth and Colleen had finished. I did track Colleen, but not my two new friends and the one who had to be taken by medic. I hoped they all finished safe and were on their way home. Once the adrenaline of the race shut down, I could barely move. The pain in the race was nothing like moving one foot after the other up small curbs, stairs or just to lift a foot to move forward. *I paid to endure this kind of pain for a medal and T-shirt?* It hurt, but it felt so good to have finished alive and well. I hoped this would not take too many days to heal. Thank goodness this was my one and only marathon. Walking shorter races will have to do. More pictures taken by Danny. Stiffly walking back to the car, prying self out of car once I got home was followed by an Epson salt bath. Then posting pictures that Dan and I took in the race on Facebook. Dan walked a half marathon following me around taking pictures. He took a lot of great shots – my personal photographer. I took pictures while in the race. So, on Facebook the album was a blend of walker and spectator perspective. With the excitement of this marathon, I purchased every professional shot.

"Since you just did a marathon, could you walk with me?" Elaine tapped me on the shoulder. "I am training to walk the Susan G. Komen 3-Day."

"Wow! I have always wanted to walk that myself. Every time I see the advertisement on TV,

I want to do it. But I can't afford the $2,300 they want to walk that."

"So, will you?"

"Sure, any time."

Elaine, a fellow member of the Cleveland Church of Christ, and I walked together, and we walked with others on organized 3-Day training walks. She was walking because of someone in her family who was affected by breast cancer. On those organized walks, I heard others' stories of why they walked – because of family members, coworkers, friends, and many because they were survivors themselves. The more I heard the more I wanted to take on this sixty-mile walk in three days. I was already marathon-trained but raising $2,300 was not my cup of tea. The challenge of sixty miles had me salivating. That was almost like three marathons in three days.

"I want you to do this walk," the Holy Spirit told me.

"What? How? Where is the money coming from?"

"Train and it will come."

I signed up and the training began. Using e-mail, Facebook, door-to-door letter drops in my neighborhood and U.S. mail the solicitation began. I walked for Maggie, the one who helped me trained for the marathon.

During the organized walks I met many new friends; four are still my friends today: Kevin, Judy, Michele and Polly. Kevin was one of the group leaders who conducted the walks. It was always fun being with him. Even though he was a male in the sea of women, he was cheerful, funny and informative about how we needed to prepare for this distance. He wore loud pink outfits and zany socks to go with the 3-Day theme. His favorite outfit was a loud neon green wicking T-shirt that read on the back: "Does this fanny pack make my butt look big?". His blue fanny pack covered in 3-Day buttons of many sizes and colors with two red water bottles was wrapped around his waist. His wife, Judy, was a cancer survivor. She walked at one time but turned to volunteering instead. He walked; she served. It was a great combination. We also had Boy Scouting leadership in common. We were members at different times, so we missed serving at the same time.

I met Michele and Polly June 16, 2012 at a training walk in North Chagrin Reservation. This was the first three-day walk for Michele and me; Polly was the pro. She had done many walks as a walker and a volunteer for many years. The three of us were fast walkers; we literally became fast friends forever. Years later we still walk two to three times a month on Saturdays together for a minimum of six miles. Every Christmas we do a seasonal walk. We walk six miles in a mall or outside if weather permits and then eat at a restaurant to celebrate Christmas and our friendship. I can rely on them to walk long miles with me when training for a long-distance race.

Walking sixty miles in three days is no joke! I would like to say it was the hardest walk I have ever done; but I cannot. I loved it! This walk and the marathon done in the same year made me realize I love walking long marathon-like distances. The marathon I thought was my bucket list one-time walk was the first of many. Walking marathons became what I enjoyed most. The first day we walked about 22ish miles. I ached and had "the walk" like finishing a marathon. *Am I going to be able to get up in the morning and walk another 20ish miles again and then again?* Each day it happened, 21ish miles the second day and 17ish miles the last day. All these walks start with lots of miles on the first day, the second day is less but over twenty and the last is the different of the two days. It depends on the city's route. No blisters plagued my feet even when we were caught in the rain on the last day in the middle of seventeen miles. By the end of the walk, it was dry and hot. During those miles I saw tons of blisters on many feet for all kinds of reasons: untrained feet, improper shoes or socks, wet feet, stuff put on feet, just because and other reasons. I thanked God for no blisters, just the normal soreness from torn muscles.

The miles, the people, the stories, the weather, the whole experience is too much to write about. What was most amazing was how God raised the $2,300 to walk. He raised $2,425! This was done within two and a half months! I started this walk late in the training season, but God did it well before it was due for me to walk the sixty miles. If someone gave me a check for $2,300, I would do this every year. God's glory shone through for me and others by taking on this challenge, that only He could do!

The next year I crewed. That means I volunteered as part of the Safety Patrol. We made sure only participants were allowed on base camp. I oversaw a van and transported our crew here and there. The most fun was being able to check out the route for various reasons. With people from our crew we would cheer on walkers as they passed. I took pictures. Michele walked with Kevin. Polly also crewed as part of one of the food pit stops for walkers. She and I both felt "left behind" watching our friends walk. That was my last year to crew. I said if I were involved again, I had to walk. Being in the field was the way to go.

The next year I did my last 3-Day in San Diego. Cleveland was no longer one of the cities for the walk, so, I had to choose another city to walk in. In California, I had a ton of family and this was the perfect reason to choose San Diego. My father, husband and I spent a week vacationing before the walk with family and in National Parks. San Diego is the most beautiful place to walk those sixty miles. Seeing the Pacific Ocean every day and climbing hills were the best for me. Walking past La Jolla brought back memories of when Dan and I scuba dived from those beaches. If ever I got the chance to do another walk, it would be in San Diego. I met more new friends that I keep in touch with through Facebook. I am hoping that somehow at a race or some other event, I will walk miles with them again on pavement.

In both 2013 and 2014 when I crewed and walked respectively, God blew out the goal amounts again. As a volunteer it was not required to raise money, but it was encouraged. As a crew member I set a goal of $500; God took it to over $1,000 and over $2,300 for the last year.

The body has a way of telling you what your physical limits should be. What you decide to do with that information is key. I learned that I loved walking marathons. I also learned that my body needed to do only one a year. It is easy to stay half marathon trained all year round, ready to do a race at any time. It is not easy to be full marathon trained all year round. Once a year is my maximum. Other races done during the year range from 5K to 13.1 miles anytime, anywhere during the year. As of this writing the following race distances have been walked:

Distance	How Many
5K	21
4 miles	2
8K	3
5 miles	1
7.6K	1
10K	10
10 miles	1
15K	1
13.1-mile relay	1
13.1 miles	23
26.2-mile relay	1
26.2 miles	6
60 miles (3-Day)	2

My body also told me that cross training was extremely important. No longer do I hate gyms. Well, I do not like most gyms because of their layout and atmosphere. God gave me the perfect place to be, The Natatorium, in Cuyahoga Falls. It is at least a twenty-minute drive from my home by highway, but it is worth the trek. It has everything I need: group classes, indoor track, swimming pool and more. I cross train with and without weights in classes and swim with snorkel, mask and fins.

Riding my bike is a cross training I enjoy with my husband. Our favorite place to bike is on the Towpath. The Towpath is eighty-seven miles and counting. It runs from the Cuyahoga River in Cleveland south to Canal Lands Park. Once completed it will have one hundred ten miles and end in New Philadelphia, Ohio. We have thirty miles left to ride.

On one of those towpath rides something different happened. We were in Summit County and suddenly I felt lightheaded. My vision darkened like someone had turned out the lights. I felt like I was going to pass out. I almost did on the bike, but thanks to God I did not. At the time I could not understand it, it was not too hot, I was not tired. I thought I was having a stroke. We stopped somewhere took in some nourishment and finished the ride.

"Juel, you are low in B12, Vitamin D and sugar. You also need to have a high protein diet!" my doctor told me.

"What are you talking about? I get the Vitamin D living in Cleveland and maybe the B12. But the low sugar and the high protein diet? I am a Weight Watcher person! I know what to eat! Why would I be low in sugar and need protein?" I gasped.

"But have you tried to walk 1,500 miles in one year?" My doctor reminded me.

I was silenced.

In 2017 God took me over the top in miles walked: 1,500 miles. While walking these miles one dollar for each mile was raised. These were the hardest miles I have ever walked. God originally gave me a goal of 1,200 miles but changed it three months into 2017 to 1,500 miles. This meant I was behind; it took several months to catch up and finish the year with 1,500 miles walked. He raised $1,550 for HOPE *worldwide,* a charitable organization that brings hope to poor, sick and suffering people around the world.

Walking that distance changed how I ate. I had to eat twice as much protein to keep me functional. My sugar level was sixty-two when I almost passed out on the towpath. As a Weight Watcher Leader, I remember telling members the reason they did not lose weight because they weren't eating enough based on their activity level; here I had fallen into that trap and was appalled. I was not trying to lose weight; my body was trying to survive. Being a walker has taught me lessons about the importance of proper nourishment.

After the completion of the 1,500 miles, starting in 2018 my yearly miles decreased. No longer do I set annual goals of miles to be walked. No longer do I sign up for numerous races. Races can be costly. I can walk miles without paying to be in race. When I enter a race now, there is something special or interesting about that race that compels me to dive in. Some of these races are on Sundays; I am extremely selective about Sunday races. Missing time with the body and God is not my goal. I lean towards the Saturday race when I walk one. Miles walked in 2018 were only eight hundred sixty-seven and for 2019 I had only seven hundred fifty-three miles walked.

More of my miles are now being walked in service. God gave me my dream volunteer position, Cleveland Metroparks Trail Ambassador. With another trail ambassador, we walk the trails in any of the eighteen Cleveland Metroparks Reservations. With hiking boots or walking shoes, pairs of us meet, greet, inform, provide first aid/CPR, assist park visitors and report any trail hazards. We are an extra set of eyes for the Cleveland Metroparks Police when there is danger or trouble.

Anytime anyone asks me why I walk I tell them: "It's Eric's and Louis's fault that I like marathons." I tell people their story and how God used them to encourage me into marathons. Walking marathons remains my favorite distance. However, I walk only one a year and because someone else wants to walk a marathon with me. Walking a marathon alone is no longer my desire. I walk so others can walk. Any races that are less than half a marathon I will walk alone but prefer to walk with a friend. My twenty-first and last half marathon was on October 27, 2019. Walking half marathons for the bling, is no longer an attraction for me. I was scheduled to walk my seventh marathon in May 2020 with a few who want to walk their first marathon. It is my hope and prayer that by walking, others will see God's glory in what He has me to do with my feet and that they will want to walk spiritually with Him eternally.

COVID-19 changed my training walk plan. Training for the Rite Aid Marathon was to be inside during the winter months and outside once the weather got warmer. After recreation centers, malls and other indoor fitness places were closed, I had to walk outside sooner than planned. The Rite Aid Marathon, along with another race, The Flying Pig, became virtual races because any gatherings over ten people were not allowed. I do not like doing virtual races; I like doing the real thing. Virtual races are done for the same distance wherever you want to race. You must report it when done. The condition of maintaining six feet of social distance also became an added adventure while training and deciding where to do our training and races.

Training in the parks proved to be difficult because too many people were there. Some refused to do social distancing; that was disturbing. So, Polly, Michele and I chose to train earlier in the morning before most of the people got there. Our walking conversations were limited because we maintained the distance of six or more feet as we walked. However, I got to see more of God in nature in these silent walks. Sometimes we covered our faces. I did it to protect others from me. Dan and I kept N95 masks in our home for the purpose of deep cleaning or other industrial work; but we did not use them outside. Other than for the purpose of walking, I stayed in the house. Given my asthma condition, I did not want to risk catching this virus.

The year of 2020 had become highlighted by four virtual outdoor races unforeseen when the year began. One of those was a half marathon after I said I was done with half marathons. However, because we were walking twelve training miles anyway, Michele and I increased it to do a Stay Home Inaugural Half Virtual Marathon due to COVID-19.

Even though I knew my seventh marathon was going to be special, I did not anticipate just how much. The seventh marathon was supposed to be the race to help people reach their goal of walking a marathon or achieving another. However, all those who said they wanted to join me changed their minds for various reasons before COVID-19 arose. I was not happy, but knew God wanted me to walk alone with Him and it would be alright. Walking alone with Him is pleasant and sweet.

However, Lou turned out to be the person He added. Lou is the one I mentioned earlier who encouraged me to walk marathons. He had to walk two virtual marathons: The Canton Football Hall of Fame Marathon and The Rite Aid Marathon. These would be his thirty-fifth and fortieth marathons.

On the day of his first virtual race, neither of us were one hundred percent healthy due to physical issues. However, in any race, Lou always pushed through whatever physical issues he had and finished the race. I tell you, if it were me, I would have never made the attempts he has done while injured. Before this race, I had an ear infection, a sinus issue and a cough. The sinus issue affected the ear, which in turn affected the cough. I prayed the cough would not lead me into an asthma attack. I was on antibiotics from the doctor and I prayed I would be fine.

I wore a face mask at the start of the race. However, as I climbed the first short hill, I had problems breathing. *What?* It was not the mask; I could not breathe like I normally do. Since we were the only ones in the park at the time, I took the mask down, stayed away from Lou and then pulled it up when others came in the opposite direction. Every ascent was brutal due to insufficient ventilation. I had to learn a different way to breathe while moving uphill and relax while going downhill – opposite of my normal mode of operation. I had hope, *we can do this, slower, but it can happen.*

Just before mile eight, the leg cramps began. Water and stretching were my release; however, I was concerned because leg cramps are not normal for me. By the time we arrived at mile twelve, I could not move. Both legs were as tight as a rock. Lou never left my side; though he could not get close to help, but he encouraged and advised. I whispered a prayer, "God let me get to at least mile 13.1." Then I stood up, stretched, and said in a low whisper "one foot in front of the other". I walked in pain, but I walked. God enabled those muscles to soften enough to continue until I could meet my husband at the rendezvous point and finish 13.1 miles.

I had made several Facebook posts along the way so that others watching knew where we were. I thought, B*ummer! Now I am going to have to tell everyone I had to quit.* I have never quit in any race. I have always finished. My dad had instilled in me "a quitter never wins, and a winner never quits". Amazingly, even though I could not finish I was thrilled God pushed me through. I did not do that last mile and one tenth alone. He had Lou coaxing me and God's strength empowering me. I posted this message with my finish time and a picture in Facebook: *"Thank you, Jesus! Despite having sinus and breathing issues, an ear infection and leg cramps like I have never had before in any race, God enabled me to make it to at least 13.1 miles. Lou is finishing the race on his own with God guiding him. This is the first time ever I did not finish a race, but I am so grateful I got halfway done. At that point, my husband and I are the support crew for Lou."* Lou's second half was faster without me.

Five of my six marathons were completed with others. I will always enjoy watching the tears of joy on their faces when they finish their first event or beat their last marathon time because God had me there walking with them. I will never forget this last marathon attempt where God was there for me to complete the roughest 13.1-mile race. There was no completed full marathon, no personal best to take home and, who knows, maybe no medal. Normally if someone does not complete a full but does a half marathon instead, they sometimes give the half marathon medal. But since this was a virtual race, who knows. I am good with that. My joy comes from knowing that my God kept me safe, helped me finished 13.1 miles, and brought me home. My truest joy will be when I am "at home" with Him eternally at the end of my life's race.

CHAPTER SIXTEEN

THE RETIREE

*"The LORD said to Moses, "This applies to
the Levites: Men twenty-five years old or more
shall come to take part in the work at the tent of
meeting, but at the age of fifty, they must retire
from their regular service and work no
longer. They may assist their brothers in per-
forming their duties at the tent of meeting, but
they themselves must not do the work. This, then,
is how you are to assign the responsibilities of
the Levites." Numbers 8:23-26.*

I hated being an IRS Agent. I could not wait
to retire and be done with this position. In the last
few years before I was eligible to be retired, God
gave me the job of Tax Computation Specialist. I
prepared the tax adjustment reports for IRS
Agents. I loved this job!

*Maybe I will stay a little longer. This is a
gravy job and I feel like I am really being of service,* I thought and told someone aloud.

"No, Juel; your date is April 1, 2011," the Holy Spirit told me. I could not argue with that!

"Is that really your retirement date or an April Fool's joke?" one of my coworkers asked.

"Yep." I answered my coworker.

"Sure sure! We'll see. I just don't see you leaving. Why not stay another three years to get 40 years in? Then your check will be so much larger."

"Nope, God said 2011. Besides, I don't want to stay another three years. I have things to do when I get outta here, places to be."

I couldn't wait to do those things work prevented me from doing – travel without taking leave, hikes in the middle of the day, working more Weight Watcher hours, training for a marathon, reading, sleeping, whatever I wanted to do when I wanted to do it.

"I am going on vacation for a couple of weeks, could you fill in for me while I am gone?" one of my coworkers at Weight Watchers asked me. She knew that it was my first week of retirement from the IRS and that I was open.

"Sure."

This coworker worked full-time at Weight Watchers; I worked part-time a few meetings here and there because of my full-time government job. I was looking forward to working more hours at a job that I had a passion for.

For two weeks I was in my car here, there and yond at various Weight Watcher meetings. Working full-time was not what God needed me to do.

Part-time was good enough. I had always said, "If this becomes a job and not a passion, it is time to go." Working full time anywhere would turn into a job. I was retired; I did not need a job. Three years later God directed me to leave Weight Watchers as an employee for another of His purposes. I remain a Weight Watcher's lifetime member to keep a healthy weight by weighing in once a month.

I continued to work my Premier Design business as a jewelry consultant. With more open hours to work it, I hoped to build it up. Soon I was running all over the place to various shows and events; it turned into a job. It was time to let that go completely. However, I still wear and buy the jewelry.

"Where are you going today?" my husband asked me as I zipped up my fanny pack.

"I am taking a hike with the Metroparks. Now I get to do those day hikes they have listed in their brochures, that work kept me from."

"Enjoy! Soon I will join you when I retire."

The first six months of retirement, I hiked, joined in various day events and other day doings, worked Weight Watchers and Premier Design. "This is too much! I am beat!" I told Danny. "I need to sit down and figure out what I want to do for the rest of my life." I was doing everything I thought I missed while I was working. I also trained and participated in a 10K and a half marathon in preparation for a full marathon in May 2012.

A girlfriend from church, Elaine, for years had talked to me about joining Bible Study Fellowship (BSF). This was an international organization that conducted in-depth Bible studies from September to May. She attended one in Bedford on Tuesday evenings. Because of my hectic work, school and family schedule I was unable to attend. As soon as I retired, I joined September 2011 at the Bedford location where she was. However, God made it noticeably clear that was not where he wanted me to be. I was retired; I did not need to go to an evening class when I could attend one in the daytime. A transfer was immediately made to a location at Riverview Church in Novelty on Wednesdays at 9:10 a.m. Bedford was closer to my home but attending in the day worked better for my new lifestyle.

I loved it at Novelty. I joined when we were studying the book of Acts. Each week I read the scripture passage for the week, answered the questions for those scriptures, discussed the questions with a small group of fifteen, listened to the lecture from the teaching leader of the class and then read the notes that applied for those weekly scriptures. This four-part way of in-depth study of the Bible is excellent. I began to see more of God and His purpose for me in these studies. Soon I was volunteering as a hostess. This was like being an usher at church, one of my favorite roles to do at church. With years of experience working with children through Boy and Girl Scouts, I no longer had the patience I did when I was young, so volunteering to work in the children's program was not an option for me. However, I did volunteer to sit with the leaders' children for fifteen minutes while they prayed before each class. I got there so early anyway, it was a perfect fit for me and the class. This did not involve any advance planning for me, just a time of play.

During the first months of the class I felt God calling me to another volunteer opportunity in the class. I thought about how exciting it would be as a group leader of one of small groups. I knew if that is what God wanted me to do, it would happen. The second year, he called me to be an administrative leader, not a group leader. I was good with that. Working behind the scenes, paperwork, setting up chairs and welcoming ladies every week was like an extended version of being an usher. For three years I loved this role and thought this was where God really wanted me to be. However, that thought about being a group leader kept nagging in my brain, especially when there was a need for more group leaders in our growing class. By year five I became a group leader. I am now in my fourth year of being a group leader. Each group of fifteen has been hand-picked by God through prayer. Each group has been and still are wonderful opportunities to build relationships, share God's attributes, share His Word and pray for each other as we experience the dramas in our lives with God.

Attending BSF has deepened my relationship with God, His Word and has given me more purpose for what He needs me to do. With an open schedule that I could fill with whatever, attending these classes helped me to see that I needed God to direct my daily doings. During my morning quiet times with Him, I pray for direction on my schedule – what needs to happen or not happen. Allowing Him to direct my schedule daily has removed the stress that I put into my schedule by doing whatever I want, which caused me to be overwhelmed and exhausted. My schedule became His and under His power, not mine. Under my power I am weak; under His power I am strong.

In March 2014 a grandson, Patrick, Jr., PJ for short, joined our family. With a thirteen-year gap between Kiara and PJ, my daughter and son-in-law needed some help with childcare. The cost of day care and not wanting to give a newborn to strangers was not appealing to Patrick, Tia nor myself for that matter. I am grateful that when both of my children were born someone in the family was available to care for them before the preschool days. I was not able to help with Kiara when she was born because of my busy life. As a retiree I was able to fill my time with watching PJ. At first it was five days a week when Tia went back to work. God must have known that five days a week would get to be a bit much for me, so he changed Patrick's job. He worked five days a week; two of his off days were during the weekdays; therefore, I watched our grandson three days a week.

He and I were everywhere together. While I trained for walking races, I pushed him in a jogging stroller with and without friends. We rolled hundreds of miles every year until he decided he did not want to ride in the stroller anymore. One day he jumped out of the stroller and pushed instead. If grandma was walking, he wanted to walk. With one of my regular walking buddies, he walked three miles of the eight miles we walked in a mall in the wintertime. He refused to get back in the stroller.

PJ grabbed his feet when we were done.

"Yeah, dude, your feet hurt from walking three miles!" I laughed.

From then on, I stopped taking him on walks with friends. I had to walk short one and a half mile distances with him at his pace, which was slow. Sometimes we would run some of that distance. He loved it – walking and running with grandma. I did, too. However, I missed the resistance of pushing him around in a stroller.

Once a week, he and I spent time in a pool for lessons. At the age of six months, my husband and I put him in a local swim class. The first year, I had to be in the water with him. That was an excellent workout walking back and forth in the water with him as he worked on whatever skill they were teaching him. He loved being in the water and having grandma with him was even better. However, I was thrilled when he got old enough for me to sit on the opposite side of the glass and watch him learn with a group of others his age. It took so much time to get us both dressed and undressed for class; without me involved getting ready was a snap. He enjoyed that class for about three years. Soon, it became apparent he was tiring of the class structure for some reason or another. He liked doing what he wanted to do when he wanted to do it.

It was probably his grandparents' fault. Dan and I during those early years took him to another pool where the water was eleven feet deep. We encouraged the lessons he was taking while at this other pool, but we would also put a life preserver on him, and we would end up in the deep water doing whatever we did. Many times, all three of us would jump from the side of the pool into the water. He loved that – jumping into the deep water. All the water was deep for him! The class was four feet deep and the shallow end of the eleven-foot pool was four feet deep. He never knew what it was like to stand in shallow water until he was four years old at a third pool, which I took him to occasionally and took a swimming lesson. It was funny watching him adjust to walking into shallow water and then swimming out to the deep water the first time. He did not know what to make of this pool of water. I wish I had been able to get that on video.

Now my days with our grandson are less because he is in kindergarten. I miss these times with him. I can tell he does, too. So, I make efforts to see him as much as I can when God enables. We have a special bond. However, I did pick him up three days a week after school until COVID-19 sent him home to schooling online.

With my granddaughter in college, I was given the pleasure of seeing her two to three days a week. Driving her to and from college was added to my schedule as PJ was being weaned out of my schedule. God's timing is perfect. Now I became grandma transport.

In addition to driving here and there with the grandchildren, exercising, walking, and visiting my two aunts once a month, God gave me a child the same age as PJ to transport from her preschool to her sitter's home while her parents worked and later from her elementary school to after care. Her mom, a fellow disciple at church, was driving from downtown every day to pick up the child, drop her off at a sitter and then drive back downtown to work. I do not know how she did it. God, however, told me I could do that for her instead. My schedule was open Monday through Friday at that right time this transport was needed. That was not normal; rarely do I have a consistent open spot every day, but I did for them. Therefore, grandma transport expanded to my spiritual family. Just before this happened, I had prayed for a source of income to help me pay cash for gas. I hated using my charge card for gas usage. With this arrangement, I was able to pay cash for gas expenditures. God knows how to provide a way.

My life as a retiree is ever changing, ever full and never dull. With God's hand in the schedule it works. I get to do what I enjoy yet am given times of refreshment to rest and begin anew. I get to interact with people for fun and in service. I get to watch how God transforms the impossible to the possible and see His glory in my comings and goings.

I have learned in these nine years, that retirement is not a time to do nothing. It is a time to be even more than what I was while working. It is a time to be more productive, joyful, physically and spiritually fit. It is freedom. Nothing in the Bible talks about retirement except for the Levities. Even with the Levities the retiree helped guide their younger brothers; they did not go home, and twiddle thumbs all day.

I have often said, "You must have a plan for what you are going to do for the rest of your life after retirement. A plan to do nothing but sit at home is a quick way to the coffin. Keeping it moving until God says stop is the way to live."

COVID-19 gave new meaning for me as a retiree. My busy penciled paper schedule became a blank erased, empty book. Though it was emptied it was refilled with ZOOM church, BSF, Board and family meetings, video chats, and walks in the park or in my neighborhood. Because of my asthma, I did not leave the house except to walk. My lunch dates to see my dad ceased; we had daily telephone or video chats instead. Keeping it moving inside my house continued as I followed God's new schedule for me. Only God knows where He is taking me during and after this pandemic as a retiree. I am confident that His plan will be best for me.

CHAPTER SEVENTEEN

THE SINUS AND ASTHMA SUFFERER

"Therefore put on the full armor of God, so that when the day of evil comes, you may be able to stand your ground, and after you have done everything, to stand." Ephesians 6:13.

"Dan, I don't want to do this, but I need to go to hospital right now!"   I gasped between breathes.

"Are you sure?"

"I was hoping this was nothing, but I can barely speak. I only ate three bites of this dinner because I can't breathe." Slowly the words came out. It seemed like I was making a long speech just to produce those two sentences.

How could I be having shortness of breath? I have not done anything today except be at home sitting on my butt! The 10-minute ab workout and 30-minute walk in my house was a good four hours ago. Besides neither of them should have had me panting like this.

"You know this means I have to walk in there alone," I gasped.

"I know." Dan said, almost in a whisper.

We rode to Ahuja Hospital in silence. Talking was too difficult. As we rode, I sent group texts to the Abigail women, my small church group, my immediate family, and a few other individuals who needed to know what was happening and to pray for me.

It was Tuesday, May 12, 2020. I was supposed to be in a Zoom meeting with fellow walker friends at 7:30 p.m. to catch up. They were the first ones to whom I sent a text. I was hoping I could hold out and go to the hospital after our time together; but when I tried to set up the computer, I felt a light headedness that should not have been there. My body felt like it was primed for a nap.

At the emergency room entrance, I put on my cloth face covering. "At least now I will be tested for COVID-19," I managed to say.

Dan and I kissed. "I will call or text. I just remembered I forgot my phone charger. So, I cut the phone off to save the battery." It seems the more I could not breathe, the more I wanted to talk. I do not remember saying "goodbye". I just remember feeling sad about walking into a hospital alone, masked and concerned that I had COVID-19. I had two of the symptoms: a cough for the past several weeks and now this unexpected shortness of breath.

Do I really have this virus? I know I said if God wanted me to have this and I had to die, I would be good with that because I would then be with Jesus. But am I ready for the suffering before that and how it would affect Danny and others?

I walked in dreading the unknown. There was not a soul in the emergency room. Normally it is packed with people. The receptionist was fully encased by four white walls. Every crack around windows and seams was sealed with some sort of adhesive tape. The window between me and her appeared to be plastic. Her mask was down while I gasped out why I was there. *Is she far enough away from me? Apparently, she is comfortable with this distance since she is in a cage."*

I was told to sit, and someone would come get me. I sat sucking in air through my face covering. Wearing a face covering does not allow for freer respiration. I do not know why I did not wear my N95 mask since I was going into a hospital. I can breathe easier with that mask than a cloth one. As I was writing this, it occurred to me that neither Dan nor I thought about making me wear the N95 mask. I think it escaped us because we were so saddened about my going. That is why it did not occur to me that I had no phone charger until I was near the hospital. I could be in ER a long time. The only reason we have those type of masks in the house is because Dan is a retired construction worker. He uses them when he works now and when he works on people's homes or cares for their lawns. They were an easy purchase from

Lowe's but have been harder to find since the emergence of COVID-19.

A masked male attendant came within minutes and took me to a room.

I was asked questions about why I was there, given a heart monitor, given an IV, a fingertip oximeter, a portable X-ray, a hospital mask, an oxygen mask and had my blood drawn. Then followed questions about whether I had been in contact with anyone with COVID-19. *No, I go nowhere. I stay home most of the time. I only go out for an occasional walk or hike. Dan is the one who goes out to grocery shop. He is extremely careful with mask, gloves, using Purell Hand Sanitizer along with soap and water. He avoids crowds of any type. We do not hike or walk where there are crowds of people.*

"How did you walk in here? Your oxygen saturation level is 70 percent!" The nurse exclaimed.

"What? Are you kidding me?!" I said through my oxygen and hospital mask. "I have never been that low!"

In late fall of 2018, Dan brought me to the hospital because I could hardly breathe. I could barely walk or talk. He rolled me in with a wheelchair. My oxygen levels were in the high 80's then. *Ok, God, You have me here for a reason. You walked me in here alone without a wheelchair. Help me not to miss what you want me to learn while I am here.*

"We are going to have to give you a COVID-19 test."

"I figured that." *I knew it! I am not looking forward to the pain. Everyone who told me about that test said it was quick, but it hurt. Argghhh! Well at least I will know for sure. This cough has been going on way too long!*

"Ok, I am going to put these two little swabs in your nostrils. It might be uncomfortable," the male attendant said.

I closed my eyes. I felt something like two toothpicks laying in my nostrils. I braced, but felt nothing.

"Ok, you're done." *That's it? What was that about? No pain with that. Maybe that is the rapid one I heard about. Oh well we shall see what this test says.*

"We need to take you for a CT-scan while we are waiting for your results."

By now I was on some sort of machine that gave me a high level of oxygen directly into my nostrils instead of the emergency rescue oxygen mask. A blue hospital mask covered the tubing and my lower face. I was on a short leash. Moving off the bed was impossible.

With all the liquids going into my IV, I had to pee a lot. After the CT-scan was done, the technician let me use the bathroom which was connected to the radiology room. Then when I was back in my room, within minutes I had to go again. I pushed the nurse's button for what seemed like an eternity. No response. With street clothes still on I let it all go in the bed. *Oh, well. If I had to have an accident, the hospital is a good place to be.* The male attendant apologized profusely. He said the nurse was tied up taking blood from another patient and could not come in time. He gave me a hospital gown, hospital pants, and warm bath wash clothes. He cleaned and changed my bed.

"Good news. Your COVID-19 test is negative," a female nurse said. "However, because of your symptoms, we are admitting you as if you have COVID-19 and we will put you in a separate area. Then another test will be taken."

"Thank goodness." I said easily under the oxygen. "I know someone who had two negative tests and later it was proved she had the virus deep in her lungs. She ended up on life support and many of us prayed her back to life."

While I waited for a room, I called Danny and posted on Facebook that I was being admitted. Between texts and phone calls, I kept the phone off. Dan was able to drop off my charger with the receptionist. My charger was by my emergency room bed after my CT-scan.

It was after midnight by the time I was in a room by myself. I was still on a short leash and had to have a commode by my bed. The in-room bathroom was too far of a distance for my hoses to stretch.

It was not a restful night. I slept maybe two or three hours between vital interruptions and just not being able to sleep. Surprisingly, I was not hungry overnight despite having not eaten since 2 p.m. the day before. My dinner of three bites had been packed away by Dan when I could not eat it.

My room faced southeasterly; God blessed me with a sunrise that I took a picture of from my bed and posted with the daily scripture on Facebook. Since this pandemic had put us on lockdown, I have been posting on Facebook a scripture in an album entitled "Fear Not. Also in that album were encouraging events and other things that make people laugh despite the new reality we all were in. At 7 a.m. I prayed with Loretta. She and I have prayed together on Wednesdays for many years. This Wednesday in the hospital was no different. In fact, I needed prayer more because of where I was.

Thanks to God, I had no fear of being in the hospital or having the virus. All during the time I was there, I talked to many on the phone through texts or Facebook posts. Right after my quiet time and prayer with Loretta, I was compelled to do a Facebook live video from my hospital bed. While I was on that "short leash" machine, I let people know my status which was "all good!" My oxygen levels were at one hundred percent and had been since Tuesday night. I was breathing better and talking.

The best part for me was the meals. It is always about the next meal for me. By the time breakfast came, I was starving. This hospital allowed me to order from a menu, and within forty-five minutes the meal was served. I liked that. There was no more of that old system of eating whenever they brought it whether you were hungry or not. Plus, the food was delicious. French toast, pork sausage, cantaloupe, potatoes, chocolate milk and water slid down my throat for breakfast. Brown rice, carrots, a grilled chicken sandwich, water and chocolate pudding satisfied my lunch taste buds. Salmon, broccoli, corn, tea and angel food cake with strawberries and whipped cream completed my dinner. My last breakfast the next day was grapes, an English muffin, an omelet with sausage, bacon, green peppers and onions, ginger ale, and tea.

I never left my room. I thought I was going to be moved for various tests like in prior hospital stays, but that was in a different time. Because it was not known yet if I was COVID-19 positive, I had practically no exposure to the hospital staff. Anytime someone came in, they were dressed in a gown, mask, face shield and gloves. After they left, they took off the robe and gloves and left them in the trash by the door. I had to wear my hospital mask anytime someone came in. The hospital masks are easy to breathe through unlike the cloth one I used when I came to the hospital.

I was in a room where the staff could look in through the window to check my physical status without coming in. They only came in to do vitals, check the machine, bring my meals, or dump the commode. Otherwise I was alone. There was a television in the room, but since I watch very little TV, it was silent. My cell phone and hospital phone were my connection to the outside world. I craved my paper bible and a book. Thank goodness the bible is on my phone for my morning quiet times with God. After a time, they removed the machine and put me on regular oxygen with a longer leash. It was not long enough to reach the bathroom, but I was able to move further away from the bed.

During the afternoon, a second test was done. This was the one that goes deep into the nasal cavities. This nurse was fully garbed with the N95 mask, shield, with no skin exposed because of the possibility of blood droplets that could come from my nose. The swab device she had was curved and long. *Now here comes the pain!* I closed my eyes. Slosh! Slosh! *What was that?* I opened my eyes. The nurse was standing there with the device in her hand.

"Did you do it already?!" I asked.

"Yep, now ready for the next nose."

"Oh my gosh. That was weird." I closed my eyes.

Slosh! Slosh! *Ugh! Oh my gosh!*

"It didn't hurt, but it sure felt weird!" I told the nurse. "Everyone one tells me that the test is painful."

"Well, this device is curved and probably the one they had was a straight swab."

"Thank you, Jesus! I was all set for pain. You were quick! I just didn't like how it felt in my nose." I shivered.

"You will know the results tomorrow morning. It takes about twelve hours." She packed up and left, leaving her garb behind.

Wednesday is the only day I regularly watch TV to see "The Masked Singer". Dan and I normally tape it and watch it afterward so we can blaze through the commercials. I was bummed at first when I remembered it was Wednesday because my situation meant I would not be able to watch the recording. Dan and I decided, if I went home the next day, we would watch it then.

Wednesday we also play "Trouble" with our grandson and granddaughter on Zoom. Most of the time our granddaughter attends unless she must work at Giant Eagle. At first, we wondered if we could do this with me in the hospital. We were able to participate using my phone, our home computer and our grandchildren's computer. I was planning to just watch since I was not near the home "Trouble" board. Dan moved my pieces for me, and I was able to play. It was so much fun. It was such a close game. Any of us could have won, but our grandson slipped his last piece in and won. Neither of our grandchildren knew I was in the hospital. My daughter had to tell them both so they would not be surprised. While we played neither of them said anything about me being in the hospital. It felt like an ordinary game day. I took a screen shot of our game and posted it on Facebook.

I posted another Facebook live video right after the game to let everyone know I was waiting for the COVID-19 test results. There was something on the X-Ray and CT-Scan, but the staff did not want to discuss it with me until they knew if I was positive or negative.

Before going to bed, I attended a Zoom Midweek Women's meeting with our church. It was so good to see everyone thanks to mobile phone technology. I was surprised at how much of an encouragement my attendance was for those who were praying for me. It was one time I could not be silent and watch since many had questions. The message was about Martha and Mary being in the full presence of Jesus; and how Jesus gently interacted with both women. It was convicting and encouraging. Thank goodness I had a small notebook in my purse for this message and my other quiet times with God in the hospital.

The second night I slept longer and was not ready to wake up when the natural light invaded my room. I learned before breakfast that my second test was negative and that I would be going home. I had pneumonia in my left lung. This was my second time having pneumonia. I had it in my right lung in the fall of 2018. I was not admitted then, just given drugs and sent home. Had it not been for the threat of COVID-19, I would probably been dismissed this time as well. The floor I was on had two wings. One wing was for the treatment of COVID-positive patients, and the other wing was for potential COVID patients like me. If I had been positive, I would have been moved to the other wing.

To exit the hospital, a nurse walked me masked-up to the elevator. Then I had to take the elevator down alone and walk alone to the door where Dan picked me up. The nurses on that floor are not allowed to leave the floor while on duty and must eat all their meals there.

I thanked God for this mini "vacation" accompanied by fabulous doctors and nurses. Because of COVID-19, it is my only overnight "trip" of the year since all my travel plans for 2020 have been postponed to next year or cancelled. I continued to pray that I would not miss what He wanted me to learn and share while there. My learning came in the week after I was discharged.

The week before I went into the hospital, I was excited about returning to my Trail Ambassador duties. Even though the Cleveland Metroparks activities and programs had been cancelled, a certain classification of volunteers was asked to serve in the park. Trail Ambassadors were trained in the new way we were going to interact with people in the park with social distancing. Hilary and I went on our first hike since the lockdown on the Friday before my hospital admission in our blue uniform vest. We wore face coverings and carried other necessary items in our fanny packs. I was thrilled to be back in my blues and serving in the park. Wearing the face covering made it a little difficult to breath; but I managed to get through our two-hour hike without suffering any ill effects.

I was excited yet apprehensive about the possibility of returning to work as a hostess since dine-in service was going to be allowed in about a week. I was not eager about wearing a face covering at work and interacting with people who might have COVID-19 without knowing it. I thought if God wanted me to go back, He would make it clear when and protect me.

The first thing I learned after my hospital stay is God told me, "Slow your roll! You are going nowhere...no Trail Ambassador and no working.

Just keep your butt at home! Wait and be still!" My wanting to get back out there was more about pride than serving. I wanted to serve, but I also relished being in my official position. In addition to that the weather was crappy when we went. It was cooler than I would have preferred. I like it warm and we still had to wear gloves and layers of clothes. Hilary and I talked about this later. I told her when I return it will have to be warmer. At this point, I will return when God makes it clear when I can be back out there. The same applies for when I go back to work. I have not been called back yet and I am not sure when this restaurant will return to dine-in service.

During my week home, God compelled me to review all the devotionals I had written about my health situation during the last ten years. It is amazing what you forget or misremember.

I was diagnosed as asthmatic in 2012. During that year or the year before, my sense of smell diminished. However, I did not notice I had no smell until 2014. In 2014 I saw an ENT and he discovered I had polyps in my nasal passages and encouraged me to have them removed. He told me that I could not exercise for two weeks. This year, I was in full training for races and a Susan G. Komen 3-Day walk in San Diego. Not exercising for two weeks was impossible. I scheduled the surgery for a time late in the year when all that activity would be done.

Before the surgery, I had a conversation with my hairdresser, Avis, about the benefits of garlic in one's diet. I asked about how it has kept her son's asthma from flaring up by using a garlic syrup. I was resolved to put garlic in my diet and use the garlic syrup. I canceled that surgery. For some reason or another, I did not feel comfortable with that doctor anyway. So, I was thrilled after talking with Avis. Adding garlic into my diet was easy and I was on it for a while. She also told me that drinking peppermint tea and eating parsley neutralizes the smell of garlic in your body.

Garlic has been a staple of my diet for as long as I can remember. I just know that somehow, because of the busyness of life, it slipped out of my diet. I had no sinus or asthma issues for at least two years until mid-2016. Then I began to suffer again. In 2016, I had symptoms of pneumonia, asthmatic bronchitis, and sinus infections.

By the end of 2017, I went to a different ENT and had the polyp removal surgery. My sense of smell returned in a few weeks.

March 2018, I walked 26.2 miles in the desert in New Mexico at the Bataan. While I was there, I visited the White Sands National Park twice with friends. I remember feeling the grittiness of the sands that blew in my throat. After the long race, I began to cough. My friend, Michele who lives in New Mexico, told me that was normal and that I would be coughing up sand and dirt for several weeks. I coughed for about a month.

That cough set into motion months of visits with general practitioners, an ENT specialist, urgent care, emergency, and a pulmonologist to determine what was going on. None of the X-rays or scans showed any lung damage due to sand or dirt. Terms such as COPD were dismissed as possible causes because pulmonary function tests disproved, I had COPD. Pulmonary function tests, spirometry and methacholine challenge tests also showed that I was not asthmatic. The pulmonary doctor told me I was misdiagnosed as asthmatic years ago and removed me from my maintenance medication. Soon, when I had further respiratory issues, it was determined I am among that ten percent of patients who can pass an asthma test but still be asthmatic. Later in the year, I had pneumonia in my right lung which was fixed with medication at home. Thanks to God I never stayed overnight in a hospital during the numerous events of breathlessness I experienced.

In 2019, I had no breathing issues that warranted medical attention. However, ever since 2018, I noticed that walking long distances (ten miles or more) were difficult on my lungs. It was not enough to keep me from walking, but I could tell it was not as it was before 2018. Thank goodness I was tapering down my distance walks. Walking long distance races for medals and T-shirts no longer interested me or my body. Walking or hiking for health and being out of doors was becoming my new norm. My only lung issue in 2019 was after my third umbilical hernia operation. I told the doctor that every now and then I made a small random gasp. I was told it was because I had been blown up with air for the robotic surgery and air was being released. They also admitted they forgot to give me a spirometer that causes me take deep breaths regularly after surgery. So, I had to do it manually on my own to stop the gasps.

In 2019 my maintenance dosage was reduced because I was doing so well. Because of peak fitness, asthma is kept at bay.

Mid-March 2020 after gyms, malls and other indoor places were closed, my activity level diminished. Because of obvious coughs, an ear infection and respiratory issues, my maintenance medicine was increased to what it was in late 2019.

As an athlete, after a long race, I tend to take ibuprofen to ease the pain of torn muscles. It is also great for fever. In April 2020, I used it three times with negative effects. The first time was for muscle pain. Later that day I had terrible abdominal pains and soft stools. It took hours to calm down. In another instance, I had a fever of 102 and used it hoping I did not have COVID. That night, everything I ate came out of both orifices all night yet brought the fever down. The third time I was feeling a strange kind of way and took it. Later that same day, I was breathless and in the hospital.

After those three situations happened within one month that included the hospital stay, I did some research on ibuprofen's effect on asthma. What I learned is that there are possible negative effects such as wheezing, shortness of breath, nasal polyps, skin rashes, nasal allergies, coughing, running nose and hives for people with asthma. Most of these symptoms I have had over the years.

The nasal polyps concerned me the most. It made me wonder. Since there is no way of knowing at this point about ibuprofen's influence, I no longer use it at all. Anytime God shows me something three times, I pay attention.

Four weeks after being discharged from the hospital I was readmitted into the hospital for a four-night stay on a regular patient floor because my oxygen level would not rise above 89 along shortness of breath. Because of my medical history a plethora of tests were done including counsel with an experienced pulmonologist. After this discharge I had my first appointment with Dr. Robert W. Hostoffer. D.O. That appointment revealed that I am allergic to English Plantain, Giant and Short Ragweed, Alternatia, Cat, Dog, D. Farinae, and D. Pteronyssinus (latter two are dust mites). Further testing will be done to determine if I have Aspirin Exacerbated Respiratory Disease (AERD) also known as Samter's Triad or Aspirin Sensitive Asthma. This could explain my ibuprofen negative reactions. Because of all of this I may not be asthmatic, but have been experiencing asthma like symptoms because of allergens and lung infections

The two times in the hospital has reminded me to return to using garlic in my diet and other natural methods of healing. I have always hated using drugs and have fought doctors about the use of drugs. I only use a drug for a short time. I have seen the awful effects of steroids on my mother and do not look to drugs as a permanent cure all. I have called doctors legalized drug pushers. It starts with one drug, then another to offset the side effects of the first drug and then years later a patient is on several drugs they are unable to withdraw from. I hate to say this, but I am not always sure that because of my skin color I received the best quality care. Proper diet is the remedy for continued good health.

This also put me on notice to improve the cleanliness of our home and keep allergens at bay. An attack plan was put in place to remove dust collecting items and to use natural nontoxic products to keep our home clean.

God created wonderful bodies for us to use for all our days. We are to protect them with proper nutrition and exercise so that the Holy Spirit can reside inside bodies full of health and energy.

I do not know what the long-range effects will be of my returning fully to natural methods of healing; but I know it will be good with God's guidance. May these latest experiences of breathlessness in the hospital be my last. Instead, may I continue to have strong lungs and nasal passages that smell the sweetness of life.

CHAPTER EIGHTEEN

THE AFRICAN AMERICAN

"'For I know the plans I have for you,' declares the Lord, 'plans to prosper you and not to harm you, plans to give you hope and a future.'"
Jeremiah 29:11.

There is one life that I was born with and that life will be with me until the day I die. That life is being an African American. I cannot run from it. I cannot change it. I can only be. God made me what I am. I have been called "Colored", "Negro" and "Black". I am a descendent of Africa.

Before I could read and write, it was engrained in me by my parents, relatives, and neighbors that I had to be the best I could be. The best I could be meant excelling at more than one hundred percent. In the world where I was growing up, one hundred percent would never be enough. I would have to work twice as hard to be extraordinary, to be respected, admired, and make a decent living. My appearance, my diction, my posture, my attitude, my dress, and my hair always had to be on point, especially in the workplace. Wearing rollers in my hair and talking like a "dumb nigga" was unacceptable.

"Racism" was not a word I thought of as a child nor with which I became familiar with until I was old enough to read and write. However, I knew what it was because it was something I lived with from the womb. It was something I could not get away from no matter how I wanted to hide from it. It always found me.

Hearing the stories from my parents, grand-parents, and other older people about what challenges they went through made me grateful I was born when I was. I was not sure how I would have endured the mistreatments and death endured by generations before me.

Despite the lessons my parents and others taught me to be the best I can be, I often have moments of insecurity about being accepted by people who are not of my race: white Americans. Part of my norm was growing up with race riots, lynching, discrimination, name calling, disrespect, belittling, civil rights backlash, assassinations and more. In addition, there was the mistreatment within my own race if you were not the right shade of brown. The lighter you were and the straighter your hair, the more likely you were of being accepted and treated better by the white race. Both African Americans and white people would chastise me about "talking too proper" and "trying to be white". I was passed over for many promotions because of what I looked like. Every day I must live two identities – the one that is acceptable by my race and the one that is acceptable by white people. That means talking two languages and exhibiting two different behavior patterns yet be pleasing in God's sight.

I do not remember my first encounter with racism, but there were many. As a woman, I did not feel the same level of discrimination as my male counter parts, but I was never allowed to forget that I was not white. Our young men are taught how to behave when among white people, especially police officers. No man was to argue, even if in the right, with a police officer. Hands must always remain visible when stopped by a law enforcer. If one had to move his hands to get a driver's license, one had to say, "I am reaching for my license, which is in my wallet, which is in my pocket." Or he must tell where the license is. Statements must be spoken out loud before any movement so that it would be understood what the young man was trying to do. So, he would not be mistaken for attempting to grab a weapon. Yet many died or were arrested anyway. Every African American man I know has been stopped many times in their lifetime by a police officer while driving a car or walking in a neighborhood and questioned.

Anytime I was pulled over by a law officer was due to obvious traffic violations except once. One day I drove to a northwest side suburb for a bible study. I arrived in the area too early to meet at the house where the study was. So, I drove

234 · JUEL A. FITZGERALD

around the neighborhood stalling for time. At a traffic light I saw police lights flash behind me.

What had I done? I wasn't speeding. Maybe I was driving too slowly.

"Where are you heading?" the officer asked me.

"To a bible study." I told him what street. "I am too early, so I was driving up and down the street stalling for time." *Oh! Oh! I am being profiled. I am in a predominantly white neighborhood.*

"I need to show you something. Could you step out of the car."

"Sure," I said with a smile. *Oh crap! Outside the car. Why? We are on a main street.*

"Look at your rear license plate."

I looked. *What am I looking for? The expiration tag was timely.*

"See how rusty it is. A police officer is not able to read that plate. You need to get new one. I am giving you a ticket for a rusty plate."

"Ok, I am sorry. I didn't know." I slowly slide back into the car trembling.

My friends from this city has repeatedly apologized for that encounter which cost me a hefty ticket and the cost of new plate at a time when I had no funds. Dan helped me pay for it. Dan was furious!

Our family loved to travel by car to faraway places. Train, plane, or bus was not an option because of cost or the inability to gain access to such transportation. Car was the best way to travel. For any trip, my mom would pack and cook food for the road. Fried chicken, potato salad, vegetables, fruit, potato chips, water, Kool-Aid, lunch meat sandwiches and more were packed in the car. We had to have enough to make the entire trip. We knew stopping at a restaurant or any eatery was not happening. In addition to the cost factor, we knew we would not be allowed to eat at any place. There were plenty of eateries with signs that read "Coloreds Only" "Whites Only." Even if we were allowed, the service was lacking and the tension in the air was too thick to stay. We stopped only at roadside rest stops and sometimes had a picnic lunch at tables or in the car. It depended on the atmosphere of the rest stop. I do not remember doing this, but my dad told me about how sometimes they had to pee alongside the road since they could not pee in a public bathroom.

Danny tells numerous stories about how when he was growing up, he was either chased or had to fight white boys while living in Maple Heights. They were often verbally abused when swimming in the pools or at events. When he lived in Maple Heights African Americans could live in one section of town of eight streets which were hemmed in by industry and railroad tracks. Only two other streets outside this area African Americans lived.

My first trip to California with my parents was memorable. This was to be our first time driving for several days in one direction. We drove South on I-7I to I-70 West and probably stopped in St. Louis our first night to stay with family, visit the "Gateway to the West" and gaze up at The Arch. We then probably took I-44 West to I-40

West to California. I was a teenager then, so I do not remember the exact route. Dad taught me how to read maps and I was his navigator. Every night we stayed at a different motel where there was a "vacancy" sign. In the short panhandle of Texas my dad stopped at several motels with vacancy signs. The clerks all said, "no vacancy here." Besides the vacancy signs you could tell the lots were not full. I do not remember how many stops he made, but we got the message "you are not welcome here." We had to drive deep into the night into the neighboring state before we were able to lay our heads down. My dad never said a negative comment about the rejections, but I could feel his rage, his hurt, and humiliation with his family of four in the car.

When I became a government paid adult and was sent to Texas for a training, Dad went with me. We stayed in a swank hotel. I said to dad, "Isn't this great! We *finally* get to stay in a hotel together after all these years and someone else is paying the tab."

He looked at me and cocked his head. "Huh? What are you talking about?"

"Remember that time we couldn't stay in Texas because of our race and had to drive to the next state to find a room? Now we can stay in a room in this state."

"Umm. I don't remember that." He got silent and it was never discussed again.

We traveled often to North Carolina where my father's family is from. One of those times Dan, our around nine-year-old son, daughter in diapers and our around seven-year-old nephew went camping there. On the Blue Ridge Parkway while driving through the park system, we stopped in a small town surrounded by a mountain. It was a town that looked the people carved a hole in the mountain and moved there.

We needed batteries. The four of us stayed in the car while Dan went into the store. The city seemed creepy to me; it was so secluded from the parkway. While he was inside people from the town saw us. It seemed as if in mass they stopped whatever they were doing and slowly started moving towards our car.

This feels like a horror movie. I thought. *Are they coming to greet us? It sure don't feel like a greeting. If they mean us harm, what I am going to do with three babies in the car and Dan in the store?* My heart raced.

Before I had any more time to think about it, Dan jumped in the car, put it in gear and off we went. I sighed with relief; I feared the ignition would not work like in the movies.

Back on the parkway, Dan said. "We had to get out of there. I asked for batteries and the guy told me flat out he didn't have any. I could see behind his head a shelf full of them. I got a bad feeling and decided we needed to split." I told him my story and we both just shook our heads.

Any time my husband and I travel, we are cautious about our destination and our route to get there. Some states are more racist than others. My husband was really concerned when we were finishing up our 50-State quest in North Dakota. He had heard many negative things about African Americans living there and we made sure we did not take any isolated back road adventures.

During this same trip, while in the state of Wyoming, we met my pen pal, Cheryl, and her husband, Mike, from Idaho. Our original plan was to stay in Idaho with them after we left Utah on our way to Washington State. However, after our car was vandalized while parked in a hotel lot in Salt Lake City that resulted in half of our belongings being stolen, we had to stay an extra night. We consequently missed staying with them because we needed to be in Oregon by a certain date. So, we changed our plans to include them meeting us in Wyoming. At that time, we were heading south from Montana to see Yellowstone National Park and The Grand Tetons National Park. The four of us stayed two nights in different hotels. Dan and I stayed in a high-end hotel which cost more than we preferred to pay. But we thought the higher cost was worth feeling more secure than we would have in a lower-rated, generic hotel. My pen pal and her husband are white. She and I have been penning for more than forty-eight years. During that excursion, we saw both parks as couples and dined in restaurants as couples.

After we had dined in one restaurant, Dan said, "I am so glad Cheryl and Mike were with us."

"Why? It was a nice place. I am glad they were there too." I said.

"I mean, we would not have been able to eat at that place, if we had been by ourselves." He added.

"Oh yeah, I know." I said softly.

Entering the restaurant, Dan and I were asked if we had a reservation. The restaurant was half empty; we saw the "look", we felt the tension. When they learned we were with two white people smiles were all around by the staff and we gained access to eat there. We would not have picked that restaurant on our own. It did not feel safe. The food was delicious. We were grateful God changed our plans that resulted in this extended stay with our friends in an area where there were very few African Americans.

I love to travel, but when we leave our country, we enjoy it even more. We enter mini Utopias where everyone is friendly. We have fun with strangers and become longtime friends with many. That "look", that tension, is rarely felt.

While on a mission trip to Indonesia with five other ladies from church, we walked a short time around Jakarta. Several of us who were not white felt like rock stars. There are not many African Americans in Indonesia. People smiled, pointed, talked among themselves as we passed and followed us as we walked. Several of them intentionally walked in front of us and took selfies with us in the background – a reverse photo bomb. There was a guy at one of the restaurants who asked me how he could have his hair styled like mine. His hair was straight black. I had no idea how to answer him, but I explained briefly how mine was done. I knew he would need a special tool or some other method to style his. I have seen other races with locs and have wondered how they were able to fix it that way.

In any case, I have found less racism overall in my travels outside the United States. We must deal with issues like any other traveler, cultural differences, and crime. I love my country and would not want to live anywhere else despite the negative treatment we are subjected to because of others beliefs we are an inferior race.

Often there are reports of African American men being unjustly killed by law officers or non-African Americans for various reasons. Each time a report happens, I am angered. I feel helpless because there doesn't seem to be anything, I can do to change it. Like anyone else who is struggling, I pray, even though no amount of praying has stopped the violence.

During the months of this COVID-19 pandemic, two African American men were killed. An unarmed man named Ahmaud Arbery was shot on February 23, 2020 while jogging in the majority white neighborhood where he lived. The claim of his perpetrators was that he supposedly fit the description of a thief and was therefore a justifiable target. On Monday, May 25, 2020 George Floyd was choked to death in Minneapolis by the constant pressure of a law enforcement officer's bended knee against the side of Floyd's neck while the victim was handcuffed behind his back and lying face down in the road. Both situations caused people to protest in various ways. For Arbury, many walked or ran 2.23 miles on May 8th to commemorate the day he was killed. May 8th was also his birthday. For Floyd, organized protests, which began peacefully but erupted into rioting, were held in many cities around the country. The shooting death of Breonna Taylor due to an illegal entry into her family home added to the tension.

Mothers of African American boys are always concerned or in prayer for the safety of their young men. As I type this, I think about my husband, my son, my grandson, my brother, my father, and any other male figure in my life. Will their demise be by the hand of another because of race, or will they live out the privilege of eventually succumbing to natural causes as we all hope? That thought is always in the mind of every African American woman and man. What needs to happen to change this injustice? I do not know.

I pray that somehow, someday there will be a generation where racism is no longer an issue. That might be a pipe dream because if the issue is not racism, it is something else: economics, social class, or some other human context that provides a false sense of superiority for those for whom these systems were designed at the expense of disenfranchised citizens. While we live in this sinful world, evil will exist until Jesus returns.

I pray that during this COVID-19 reality, many will come to know Jesus as their Lord and be transformed into the beings God meant them to be: loving peacemakers living to do God's will.

CHAPTER NINETEEN

THE DISCIPLE

"Then Jesus came to them and said, 'All authority in heaven and on earth has been given to me. Therefore go and make disciples of all nations, baptizing them in the name of the Father and of the Son and of the Holy Spirit, and teaching them to obey everything I have commanded you. And surely I am with you always, to the very end of the age.'" Matthew 28:16-20.

Our eyes locked from across the parking lot. As we got closer, I realized I did not know her or her friend. She appeared to be Asian and her friend who walked with on crutches appeared to be Caucasian. *Who were these two? Why is it they look like they want to talk with me?*

"Hi, I am Susan, and this is Adela. We would like to invite you to church."

Church? I was looking for a church that was diverse. This Asian and white girl were definitely not what I was. "I am just visiting my son here. I don't live down here; so, I am not able to come to church this far away." I started to move around them. I was at Kent State to visit my son.

"Oh, we meet at the Marriott in Beachwood on hotel row," one of them piped in as they handed me a card.

"Wow! That is close to where I live. This Sunday, however, I am taking a group of Girl Scouts to Savannah, Georgia. So, I won't be able to come. But I will come the following Sunday after I come back. Thanks for the invite, gotta go." I slipped away.

They told me later that they looked at each other and one of them said. "We'll never see her again. That's a new excuse I haven't heard before."

It had been years since Dan, and I had attended church. We were baptized and married for several years. However, for some reason we both lost interest. Something was missing; we stopped going. After several years, something in me said I needed to be back in church, a church that was diverse. Churches I had attended in the past were always predominately African American. I was raised Baptist; so was Dan. Something told me, "Heaven is not all black, so why should I go to an all-black church?" The search for a diverse church began, preferably Baptist.

The following Sunday after our time in Savannah with our Girl Scout troop, I visited this church. It was held in one of the conference rooms surrounded by those folding partitions at the Marriott on Orange Place in Beachwood.

"Is there a Susan or Adela here?" I asked someone. I did not want to go to the wrong place.

"Yes, I think they are both in Kids Kingdom. I will let them know you are here. In the meantime, you can take a seat."

"Ok, thanks." *Kids Kingdom? Is that like Sunday School? I thought, oh man, I hope this is not the Witnesses. I am not interested in that. But they don't meet in hotels, so it can't be them,* I thought while taking a seat in the middle section of the rows of seats. I was early and there were lots of seats to pick from. I saved myself a seat by placing a jacket on the chair and went back to the hall where the lady said she would find the two I asked about.

"They can't come out, but I can take you to the door where they are, so they can see you." She let me down the hall to a room that was filling up with children of various ages. The one with the crutches was there, Adela.

"You came! We just knew you were telling us a story about coming. I am so glad to see you, wait until I tell Susan you came! We are both in Kids Kingdom, so we can't sit with you, but I am sure you will find someone to talk to. We'll see you afterwards."

"OK." I walked back to the room which was now starting to fill up.

Before I had a chance to get to my seat, I could see this church was diverse – races of all kinds. They were real huggy too as they greeted me and asked how I got there. I told them Susan and Adela.

"Hi, my name is Tammy. Can I sit with you?"

"Sure." I was glad not to sit alone. Tammy was closer in age to me and of the same race. We chitchatted while waiting for service to begin. She introduced me to her husband John who appeared to be Asian. *Ummm*, I thought, *a diverse couple.* Her husband might have been ushering; I do not remember seeing too much more of him that day.

Then the service began with song. The people leading songs were of many races, male and female. Speakers of various races said various things from welcome to other stuff that I do not remember. Soon the minister, Ruben, took the stage. He was black, and his wife was too. *Wow! How is that possible?* There were more non-Blacks in the congregation than Blacks. Ummm, so different, than what I was accustomed too. They all seemed so happy to be there and be with each other. I liked this.

Somehow, after the service, Tammy convinced me to study the Bible with her and someone else at my house. *Wait! Hold up! How did that happen? I don't even know her.* But I agreed to study anyway.

Tammy and Sylvia from Akron drove to my house for several weeks once a week to study the Bible with me. I was stunned by two things – that two ladies drove so far to study with me and that I was not right with God. I considered myself a Christian and knew the good works I was doing in the community with Boy and Girl Scouts were pleasing to God. Yeah, I was not attending a church, but did I really have to be a church member somewhere? The words in the Bible convinced me that I was not living the life of a Christian/disciple and a change had to occur. I confessed a slew of sins, repented and was baptized for the forgiveness of my sins on my son's birthday, November 30, 1997 at the age of forty-one years old. I considered the baptism I had when I was seventeen years old as a getting wet ceremony to be a member of the church I was attending then. No repentance of sins occurred at the first baptism, nor was it encouraged.

On the day of my baptism, which was in the basement of one of the members of the church, I was concerned about my hair. My soft sometimes curly, sometimes straight hair, depending on what chemical was in it, did not like to get wet. Wet meant it shrank tightly on my head. I wanted to be washed clean of my sins but worried about what my hair would look like for work the next day. Going to the hairdresser immediately after at night was out of the question. I talked with someone about it and I wore a swim cap to keep some of the water out; swim caps rarely keep every strand dry. After my submersion, and towel drying, my hair was a soft fluffy, shiny, curly mass afro neatness. It had never looked so good! *Gee,* I thought, *I need to be baptized more often!*

I told everyone I knew about my conversion. No one came with me to church. My daughter came because she was a minor; I dragged her there. Soon she stopped attending. My husband was not interested either for various reasons. He would come to picnics and other events but rarely to a full service. He knows all the people, sings all the songs, but it was not his time yet.

"You are in a cult!" The finger pointed at me. "You need to get out now!"

"No, I am not!"

"I am coming to check this out and decide for myself!" the voice behind the finger said.

My parents, son, family and others' fingers pointed at me soon after baptism. It was because I was not who they once knew. My aunt invited me to come to her baptism at a local church. I questioned her about this event and why she was doing it. She was doing it to confirm her membership in the church and to be saved. When I told her, I could not be part of the celebration because it wasn't a true baptism because it wasn't about repentance and forgiveness of sins, she was not happy and was hurt. I was so young in the faith and radical, I did not care. I wanted her to be baptized for the right reason. Her life never changed. The fingers and abuse came on stronger after I did not attend. Now after looking back, I wish I had been mature enough to handle that differently, but it was my conviction and I was not going to back down.

Because of the persecutions, I started to wonder if they might be right. This church was different than others I had seen or been a part of. I researched the Internet. No! No! No! There was so much negative flack about the International Churches of Christ. People accused the organization of being a cult. Oh my gosh! I might really be in a cult! How could I have made that mistake? This seems so real. How can I face my family now? There were tons of positive feedback also about the church; the negatives caused me to doubt. I did not ask anyone in the church because I feared they would make me "drink the Kool-Aid (®)" if they suspected my thoughts. So, I did the only thing I could; I prayed and opened my Bible.

A scripture jumped out at me; how I wish I can remember which one. As a baby disciple I was not accustomed to journalizing God's messages to me. Whatever that scripture was, it and the Holy Spirit softly said, "Stay, you are in the right place." I broke down in tears; I was home even if no one goes with me.

"Ummm, maybe you are not in a cult, your church does follow what the Bible says, which is a hard road to walk," my mom told me after she made a visit along with my son. They were happy with their church homes but was glad I was not in a cult. I praised Jesus that I was in the right place.

Attending church without my husband was rough. Satan knew exactly what buttons to push and he used everything he had in his arsenal to get me back into his camp. There was a term used in church, "spiritually single" for people whose spouses were not members of the church. I loved that title. However, it also made me long to be like the singles in our church. They seemed to be having lots of fun encouraging each other on dates. I wanted to be part of that. Eventually, I had to stop using that term for myself and others like me. "I

am married. I am NOT single spiritually or physically." Soon that term was no longer used in our
church. It was just another deception, from the
evil one.

As a young disciple, I attended every church
service, every midweek service, every conference,
studied the Bible with many people, attended any
and every event the church had. I spent more time
involved with church than whatever else I was doing, which meant I was not home a lot. Not being
home meant my marriage was damaged. We
drifted apart. Years later I had to learn to have
balance between church and home.

I had to learn to enjoy spending more time
with my husband. I am now at a place where Sundays are reserved for my date with God and my
date with my husband. Sunday is the best day for
us to meet and regroup after a hard week. We both
spend so much time doing so many other things
apart, that we both realized Sunday is the day for
us. Rarely do we do something else that does not
involve the other on a date on Sundays; it is un-
touchable. Sundays are a joy for me – I get time
with the body of Christ and time with the spouse
God granted me with.

Balancing home and church meant saying
"no" to church events and obligations and allowing God to direct me at what service I should or
should not provide in His kingdom. It is so much
easier allowing him to lead. With my hands on the
controls, I was overwhelmed, stressful, and lacked
peace. God's way is always best.

It has been twenty-two, soon to be twenty-three years of walking alone with God. But I have not really been alone. He has been holding my hand. He has given me many sisters in the body to correct, rebuke, encourage, teach, and guide me with His Word. He has allowed heart-wrenching experiences to mold me. He continues to teach me to be forgiving, compassionate, patient, and humble with His creation – a creation I sometimes want to strangle! He has enabled me to use the talents He has given me for His good purpose, even when I do not want to. His provision is enough; I am never in need, even when I do not have a penny in my pocket.

Juel, The Disciple, was born on November 30, 1997. The many lives in this book come and go, overlap each other, or evolve into another life. The Disciple lives through the lives that came after her and was developed in the lives that came before her. She is the unique piece of flesh made by the Creator for His glory to shine through.

If God needed me to have the COVID-19 virus and leave this existence, of all the lives, this one reigns eternally with her Lord and Savior as her identity – The Disciple, a Child of God.

CPSIA information can be obtained
at www.ICGtesting.com
Printed in the USA
BVHW071057240720
584412BV00002B/87

9 781734 858303